ACTON

A HISTORY

The Rev. William Antrobus, 1797-1853, the joint longest serving Rector in Acton's history.

ACTON

A HISTORY

JONATHAN OATES

Phillimore

2003

Published by
PHILLIMORE & CO. LTD
Shopwyke Manor Barn, Chichester, West Sussex, England

© Jonathan Oates, 2003

ISBN 1 86077 277 3

Printed and bound in Great Britain by
BUTLER & TANNER LTD
London and Frome

Contents

List of Illustrations

Frontispiece: The Rev. William Antrobus, 1797-1853

Acknowledgements

The author would like to thank the following for reading the draft and making useful comments: Mr P. Fitzmaurice, Mr J. Gauss, Miss M. Gooding, Mr D. Knights and Mrs Harper Smith. Any errors of fact or interpretation are, of course, mine.

I would also like to thank the London Borough of Ealing for the use of the illustrations in the book.

This book is dedicated to Caroline.

Introduction

Acton cannot claim to have been neglected by historians. Indeed, compared with some parts of Middlesex, it suffers from having an embarrassing amount of attention being paid to its history. In the four years prior to the First World War, there were three books written about Acton. In more recent years three books of collections of Acton in old photographs and that mine of facts that is Mr Rowland's *Acton A-Z* have been published. There is also a chapter about Acton in the seventh volume of the *Victoria County History of Middlesex*, and, on a more popular level, a chapter in Kate McEwan's *Ealing Walkabout*. Last, and by no means least, Acton boasts an active history group, which, apart from its regular programmes of meetings, talks and visits, publishes a bi-annual journal. Its members, especially the indefatigable Harper Smiths, have written a substantial number of well researched monographs on a variety of aspects of Acton's history, from sewers to stained glass windows.

It might reasonably be asked, therefore, what conceivable reason could there be for yet another history to add to those already on the shelves. It is this: there is no one account of Acton, from its prehistoric years to the late 20th century. Those books published in the early 20th century, though not without use and interest, are unsatisfactory, arranged as they are in a manner which is difficult to digest and/or containing much which is irrelevant or unreliable. Other works, though splendid in themselves, are thematic, and do not aim to be general histories. Furthermore, there has been relatively little or nothing published on Acton's history since 1914.

This history aims to fill this gap. It will deal with Acton from the Stone Age, from its origins as a Saxon village to its growth as an industrial town, and complete its story as Acton became part of the newly created London Borough of Ealing in 1965. Most of the book will concentrate on Acton's recent history, from the 18th century onwards. This is for two reasons. Firstly, because there is relatively little information about Acton's early history as a village in Middlesex. Secondly, most of Acton's major developments occurred in more modern times, principally its transformation from rural village to part of the suburban sprawl of west London. With this change came the explosion in transport developments, a huge surge in population and the rise of heavy industry. It will also try to dispel a number of remarkably persistent myths which have grown up about Acton.

As ever, the question is where to locate the sources which tell of Acton's past. There are few physical remains of Acton dating beyond the later 19th century. In 1910 Perceval Joliffe noted:

> It is true that Acton has no ancient Parish Church as a Memorial of the ecclesiastical history of the past, nor does it contain the ivy-clad ruins of a war-battered castle to remind of the exciting days

of old. No time worn inn, with gabled front, and low browed archway leading to galleried courtyard beyond, stand in the High street to speak of the leisurely times that are gone.

If this were true in 1910, it is even more so nearly a century hence.

But there are the records of the parish of Acton, both civil and religious, and the Quarter Sessions records of Middlesex, which shed light on Acton's history from the 16th to the 19th centuries. For the 19th and 20th centuries, there is the local press, primarily *The Acton Gazette* from 1871, and the records of the various councils which have governed Acton in this period. These are housed by Ealing Local History Centre at the Central Library. Especially useful are the indexes to the local press, compiled by the Acton History Group. With the aid of these sources, the author has compiled a portrait of Acton in these centuries. A full list of these sources is to be found in the bibliography.

It does not, of course, pretend to be a complete history in any sense of the word. Certainly it is not so for the last three centuries. Pressure of space has led to its being impossible to deal with every concern, let alone cover the key issues in the depth they deserve. It is hoped, though, that this book provides an overview of what appear to be the major developments, the noteworthy incidents and people; enough to satisfy the interest of the general reader and to whet the appetite of the more serious historian of Acton.

Acton, like almost every other place in England, has been spelt variously over the centuries. Surprisingly, the modern spelling was also the first known spelling in 1181; though in the 13th century it was Actone and Aketon. In the later Middle Ages it was either Aghton or Churche (or Chirche) Acton. By the end of the 16th century onwards, its spelling had been fixed at Acton. East Acton was known as Estacton in the Middle Ages.

Acton is only five miles to the west of central London, a fact that was to have no small influence on its growth in the later 19th and 20th centuries. It was a relatively large parish, consisting of 1,900 acres in the 18th century, rising to 2,319 in the 1930s. The soil in the north of the parish is clay and in the south a rich loam. Ealing is to the west, Chiswick to the south, Willesden to the north and Hammersmith to the east.

Acton's Origins and the Middle Ages

Acton's origins, like those for most places in England, are shrouded in mystery. We know little of Acton's history before the 16th century. Earlier writers often offered generalised and imaginative accounts of the place and its people which are of limited use at best. However, in recent years, the labours of the Harper Smiths have shed more light on Acton before the Reformation.

Traces of Acton's prehistory have been known about for many years. We owe much of our knowledge of the men who inhabited this part of Middlesex before records began to the work of General Pitt Rivers and John Allen Brown, two amateur Victorian archaeologists who worked in Ealing and Acton. Pitt Rivers seems to have found the earliest evidence for human activity in what is now Acton, though whether this was evidence of nomadic hunter gatherers or of more fixed settlements we cannot know. These were flint hand axes from the Palaeolithic period, about 400,000-200,000 B.C. In 1885 Brown found hundreds of Stone-Age implements, perhaps dating 10,000 years before the birth of Christ, near to where Creffield Road was later built. These were sharp flints, heads of spears and other tools and weapons. It was thought that they might have lain on what

was once an island. Evidence of Stone-Age burials has been found near Mill Hill Park. Iron-Age coins were located near Bollo Lane.

It was once thought there was a Roman camp near Friar's Place Farm, but this was probably a

1 Remains of rock left by a glacier in prehistoric times.

2 *John Allen Brown, Victorian archaeologist and discoverer of prehistoric finds in Acton.*

Anglo-Saxon, so presumably a village existed here before 1066. It used to be thought, and this story was given credence by its frequent repetition in borough guides, that the first written reference to Acton was in A.D. 716, when a Saxon charter noted the granting of land in Acton by Ethelbald, King of the East Mercians, to the Church. He did indeed do so, but it was to Acton Beauchamp in Hereford-shire (there are thought to be at least 17 other Actons in England).

What actually happened was this. In A.D. 704 the Bishop of London, Waldhere, bought the manor of Fulham from the King of Mercia and Essex. This manor included Acton, as well as Chiswick, Brentford, Ealing and Fulham itself. Fulham was the centre of this great manor and that was where the manor house was located; there were no such buildings in Acton. This has not stopped some referring to the mansion in East Acton as East Acton Manor House. One indication that the Saxon settlement at Acton must have been tiny was that there was no church here until after the Norman Conquest.

The first recorded usage of the name Acton is in 1181, since, being part of Fulham, it was not

moated mansion of the Middle Ages. Certainly, remains of pots dating from the 14th or 15th centuries have been found here. It was even once believed that Henry III had a residence at Acton, but this idea has now been discredited. Firm evidence of any Roman presence in Acton is also rather limited. Roman pottery and coins, together with a lamp and a tile of the Sixth Legion, have been located here. Most of this was found near Acton Green, to the south of the parish, not far from one of the main Roman roads leading westwards out of Londinium.

These early men were probably nomadic. A permanent settlement called Acton was, however, undoubtedly established in Saxon times, namely between the fifth century and the eleventh. The name Acton, meaning 'oak town', is

3 *Phil Philo, former curator of Gunnersbury Museum, with palaeolithic hand axe found by General Pitt Rivers.*

individually recorded in the great Domesday Book of 1086, but the Survey does include references to Acton. There were, in fact, two farms in the north of Acton. A large tract of land to the west of what was then Green Lane, but which is now Twyford Avenue, was owned by a wealthy Londoner called Fulchered, who owned, in total, several hundred acres in the manor. In Saxon times this land had been held by two tenants of the Bishop of London.

It would appear that most of Acton's arable land in the Middle Ages was divided into five common fields (East Field, Church Field, South Field, Turnham Field and North Field), in which each family farmed a number of strips of land. After 1220 the Bishop decided to take direct control of the last named field, which ceased to be common land. In 1086 there were six villagers and seven cottagers who worked these fields, perhaps making a total population of sixty people. These lands passed to the Fitz Alufs at some time, probably in the 12th century. Eventually they were held by one man, Peter Fitz Aluf (c.1170-1243), who was by now a wealthy landowner with property in Acton and elsewhere.

In the early 13th century Peter was up to his neck in debt, and in order to meet his creditors granted (i.e. sold) to Geoffrey de Lucy, Dean of St Paul's, much of his land in Acton in about 1232. The extent of this estate has been estimated at 150 acres. It included an important estate, that of Berrymead, which will be referred to again in this narrative. It also included some of the parcels of land noted in the above paragraph, which were to the west of the parish. The remainder of Peter Aluf's estates in Acton, mostly land to the north and west of the parish, were acquired by St Bartholomew's Priory in the 14th century.

Towards the latter part of the 15th century, the wealthy Frowyk family bought up land in Acton, though they actually lived in Gunnersbury, then part of Ealing. By the time of his death in 1485, Sir Thomas Frowyk, a goldsmith by profession, owned property and 70 acres of land in Acton. Some of this was left to the clergy, but most to his sons.

It is uncertain exactly what farming occurred on these lands. Arable farming for certain, but as to the crops we are unclear. The Dean of St Paul's leased some land in Willesden for a rent of wheat-meal and oatmeal; possibly similar conditions prevailed in parts of Acton. Some land was used for pasture. One of the farms leased to a number of deans in the 13th century contained oxen, horses and sheep. By the 14th century, there was a mixture of meadowland, woodland and pasture. There were a number of common waste fields where animals could be grazed. The largest was Old Oak Common, and others included Acton Green and land in north and west Acton.

As mentioned, Acton was part of the manor of Fulham, one of many held by the Bishop of London, from the early eighth century. His agent was responsible for running the manorial courts which made decisions for Acton. This business mainly consisted of the appointment of manorial officers, repairing the road and settling disputes over the quality of ale and bread. In 1232 Henry III allowed the Bishop to hold markets in Acton every Monday. This meant that the Bishop could collect fees from the traders whom he allowed to set up stalls in his manor.

The centre of the old village, called Church Acton, lay on the Oxford Road (from the 19th century onward known as the Uxbridge Road), around the parish church. There were at least two inns by the late 14th century, the *Tabard* and the *Cock*, both of which were on the main road, opposite the church. Farmhouses adjoined both the main road and Horn Lane. Friar's Place Farm was one of the latter, as was a moated site to its west. There were some outlying farms and settlements, too,

ANTIQUITIES OF
MIDDLESEX.

Montagu Sharpe. 1931.

▲ ■	Roman Survey Mounds & Stones.	Ⓜ 🍇 Moats & Vineyards.
▽ ▽ ▽	British Roman & Saxon remains. found in locality.	—— Roman Main Roads.
Ⓐ Ⓡ	British & Roman Camps.	- - - British Trackways.
⋯⋯	Boundaries of Hundreds.	

the most important being East Acton. East Acton existed from at least 1294 and originally consisted of farm houses and cottages around a piece of common land know as East Acton Green.

St Mary's church was the centre of parish life. It existed from at least 1220 (there is no reference to one being here in Domesday Book), the first known rector being Walter of Stepney. The church was valued at £13 6s. 9d. during this period. The building itself was made of flint and soft stone, with low walls and narrow windows. The altar table was made out of black marble from Derbyshire. It was a small building, as befitted a parish with a minuscule population. After enlargements in the 13th century, its length was only 80 feet.

There is a list of rectors in St Mary's and we know something about many of them. Yet most of the early rectors probably did not live in Acton, for most held senior positions at St Paul's Cathedral. After all, the manor was held by the Bishop, who lived at St Paul's. John of Fulham, rector in the 14th century, actually travelled around the country with the king as part of the royal household. The work of the parish would have been carried out instead by chaplains who lived locally. This absenteeism was not uncommon in the Church up until the 18th century, and we shall note it again in Acton's history.

Little is known about these chaplains. Some were either local beneficiaries or benefactors recorded in wills. Thomas Fighter of Acton left, in 1377, 18 pence to the anonymous chaplain (probably Adam Spencer), as well as gifts for the church. Spencer, in turn, left gifts and money to the church in 1378. Acton's church had a parish clerk of the name of Robert Hull in the middle of the 15th century. He probably assisted with the church services and parish administration.

4 Map of Middlesex in Norman times, as imagined by Sir Montagu Sharpe.

That part of the Oxford Road which ran through Acton often proved burdensome. On at least two occasions in the middle of the 14th century the men of Acton had to carry out repairs on it. The worst stretch of the road was the sharp incline just west of St Mary's, at Acton Hill. Money was left in a 15th-century will to help repair the road at this point. There were also at least three bridges in the Middle Ages. One crossed the Bollo Brook to the south of the main road, and the first reference to this is in 1239.

The Oxford Road was often used by the king and his court. In 1325 John of Fulham, Rector of Acton, was listed as one of the signatories in a royal document, indicating that Edward II and his peripatetic court called a halt at Acton on one day. It is thought they may have been travelling towards the royal castle at Woodstock, near Oxford. In the same year, the Warden and two Fellows of Merton College, Oxford, on their way to London, stopped for the night in Acton.

Apart from the Oxford Road, there were a number of trackways in medieval Acton. A track followed the Bollo Brook southwards. Heading northwards towards Harrow was Stone Lane (later known as Horn Lane). There was a footpath from East Acton to St Mary's. As previously indicated, the name Acton meant 'oak town', and in the Middle Ages this name was certainly not fanciful. Acton, like much of Middlesex – indeed of England – was heavily wooded. This especially applied to the north of the parish. Oaks and elms still existed along the roads and in private estates until the early 20th century.

Acton seems to have been a relatively prosperous place, at least for some. There was enough wealth for several medieval parishioners to leave money in their wills to the church, the poor and for repairs to local bridges and roads. There was little recorded 'excitement' here in the Middle Ages. There were no battles and the effects of the Black

Death (if any) are unrecorded. In 1340 a prisoner who had escaped from the Tower of London was re-arrested in Acton and Sir Simon Rede, brother of the chaplain, killed one of the king's enemies on the highway in 1458. He was pardoned.

By 1485 Acton, as a settlement, had been in existence for several centuries, though only the barest outline of its history is known for this period. It is probable that for most of the tiny population life did not change much over these hundreds of years. Agricultural employment on strips of common land and the Church were probably the axes around which their lives revolved, which for most were largely a matter of self-sufficiency.

II

The Emergence of the Parish

As for earlier centuries, records of life in 16th-century Acton are sparse. The parish registers, which began to be kept in 1539 (baptisms only; marriages and burials began to be recorded from 1566) following Thomas Cromwell's orders of the previous year, do, for the first time, list ordinary parishioners. These records hint at how few people resided in Acton. For example, between 1570-6, only 84 were baptised (an average of 12 per year, or one per month) and 96 were buried (an average of just more than one per month). Marriages were even less frequent; often only three or four a year in the late 16th century. Population growth was therefore slow, perhaps almost static, but probably not in decline for some of the burials were of strangers, not parishioners.

The impact of the reformation in Acton is difficult to assess. On the one hand, the Berrymead estate, for centuries in the possession of the Dean and Chapter of St Paul's, was taken by Henry VIII in 1544. He granted it to Lord Russell. By marriage it passed into the Somerset family shortly afterwards. However, the Catholic doctrine of saying mass for the souls of the departed continued here for a time, even after the break with Rome. John Byrde, Rector of Acton from 1486-1542 (Acton's joint longest-serving cleric), had the following words, which indicate he clung to pre-reformation religious practices, inscribed on his memorial brass: 'For my soul yntercede that glory yt may reyne/And for you again pray by whose charitie I am relevyed'. This should be no surprise, for he said mass in Latin during his rectorship. Towards the end of his life he saw the setting up of the first English Bible in his church, which was quite an innovation. Unlike most medieval rectors he appears to have actually resided within the parish.

Another indication of the reformation's initially limited impact was the posthumous arrangements made for Humfrey Cavell, a lawyer. Cavell, who was buried at Acton in 1558, had asked for a brass inscription to be placed on the church wall, and for a Requiem Mass to be said for his soul every week for a year. Cavell was a wealthy man, owning property in Acton and Ealing and elsewhere. He was probably one of the last Catholics in Acton for many years. After Byrde's death, Acton did not have a resident rector for several decades. Continuity, though, was provided by Simon Essex. Essex had been

5 *Monumental brass of Humfrey Cavell, 1558.*

chaplain under Byrde and continued to serve the church and parish after 1542 until his death in 1551.

The church benefited in these years by the piety of wealthy parishioners. Each of the chapels within the church had statues, including those of St Margaret and St Nicholas. Lights burned behind them, paid for by bequests. The statues were probably carved in Acton, too. It is likely that Acton lost its three altars during the radical phase of the reformation in the early 1550s.

Another long-serving and resident rector was John Kendall, who held the office from 1576-1627. He was perhaps the first of Acton's rectors not to be celibate. He had a new rectory built in which he could live with his wife, Anne, and daughters Jane and Anne. He also seems to have been an efficient rector, frequently signing parishioners' wills and ensuring accurate accounts were kept and that a proper communion collection book was maintained. It is possible there was some additional work done to the church tower in this period, but not a wholesale rebuilding of the church as stated by a brass in the modern church.

Apart from the clergymen, the parish was served by a number of officials: two churchwardens, the surveyor of the highway and two overseers of the poor. The first references to the churchwardens and overseers is in the later 16th century; there may have been no surveyor until the first part of the succeeding century. These men were appointed annually at the Easter meeting of the vestry. The vestry was a group of several ratepayers (14 assembled at the meeting in 1586), usually the more wealthy, who made up 'local government' at the time. The parish officials were also men of substance. The Child family, who owned land in the parish in the 16th and 17th centuries, often worked as parish officials, as did the Aldridges. Details of their work only emerge in the late 17th century, with the survival of churchwardens' accounts, as outlined below. Constables and ale

tasters for the parish were selected by the manor.

There were still concerns about the upkeep of the road. One Londoner evidently thought it was so dire he left money in his will in 1504 to help repair it. Although parishioners were obliged to work on the road, they often did not do so. Bollo Bridge was in decay in 1554. A newly recognised trackway, Worton Green Lane, connected Friar's Place Farm and East Acton by 1639. But Acton became less wooded in the 16th century, presumably because wood was used for housing in London and elsewhere, and for the ships of the Royal Navy. The Frowyk estate included valuable woodland up to at least 1518 but had little in later years. Another great estate in Acton also lost most of its trees by the middle of the century.

There was plenty of livestock. For each acre of land held, a man could have three sheep, two cows and a horse. Even those without land, but who possessed common rights, could keep four sheep and two cows. The agrarian economy in Acton seems to have been mixed; wheat was grown as well as animals being reared for meat. An assessment made by the constable for the controversial Ship Tax of 1635 revealed that the principal crops in the parish were wheat, hay, oats and straw. It also noted there was veal and poultry aplenty.

The number of inns increased. Apart from the two medieval ones, there were another four by the 16th century, the *Star*, the *White Lion*, the *George* and the *Hartshorn*. One which is first mentioned in the 17th century is the *King's Head*, where the parish vestry met in 1674. We know little of local recreations but bowling seems to have been popular. In 1622 there was a 'bowling place', probably at Acton Green. There was another on the south side of East Acton Mansion.

The first recorded crimes in and around Acton date back to the middle of the 16th century with the early Quarter Sessions records. Henry Follantyne, a Harrow yeoman, was attacked on the road

6 Norden's map of Middlesex, 1610.

near Acton in the summer of 1557 by George Foscum and 'divers unknown persons'. He was robbed of his possessions, including his sword and dagger, but Foscum was arrested and executed for his crimes. Thomas Brown, once an Acton miller, turned to highway robbery in 1574 and also met his just deserts. Beggars as well as robbers were a danger, and 36 were arrested in Acton in 1580. They were flogged and had their right ears branded.

The church was the recipient of a great gift. Alicia, Duchess of Dudley presented it with silver gilt communion plate in 1639. The bell ringers were paid in wine to celebrate the occasion and

there was a dinner in honour of the event, too. The Duchess' motive is unknown, but she did give similar gifts to other churches in Middlesex. Also in this era, a poor house was founded and a schoolmaster employed.

Little did Actonians know it, but this was the calm before the storm. In 1640 the constables had been asked by Parliament to report any Catholics that resided in the parish. There were none, but Catholics were supposedly, though incorrectly, thought to be in league with the King to subvert the Protestant Church. Trouble between Charles I and certain Members of Parliament erupted into civil war and Acton was briefly involved in one of

7 Church plate belonging to St Mary's, Acton.

the potentially decisive events of the conflict. It was little over five miles from the capital and straddled the road from London to Oxford. The outbreak of war in 1642 resulted in Royalists trying to gain control of the capital, the seat of administration and centre of the nation's commercial wealth, after the indecisive battle at Edgehill, and Acton lay near the route they would have to take.

Acton was briefly headquarters of the Parliamentary generals Essex and Warwick during the battle of Brentford on 12 November 1642, in which the Royalists scored a victory. This opened up the possibility that London might be taken and the war brought to an end. What happened on the following day, a Sunday, is subject to dispute. Parliament mustered troops, including the London Trained Bands, on Turnham Green and Acton Green. One account, by a Roundhead propagandist, claimed there was heavy fighting and large

casualties, especially on the Royalist side (700 Royalists to 150 Roundheads dead). A similar contemporary account referred to 'the inhuman and most barbarous actions of the Cavaliers at their entrance into Acton'. But these two accounts seem to refer to the fight at Brentford on Saturday 12 November. Others, rather more plausibly, claim that what happened near Acton was more in the nature of a stand-off, neither side wishing to commit themselves to battle. There appears to have been skirmishing when some of the Royalists contemplated a flank attack, and some ineffectual artillery fire, but that was all. What is certain is that Prince Rupert and his royalist troops retreated. Acton's parish registers record just two soldiers' deaths, and they probably died of wounds received on the previous day at Brentford.

Parliamentary soldiers billeted themselves on the town, with the Rev. Daniel Featley (rector from

1627) being turned out to make way for one Colonel Urrey. The Earl of Essex, the Parliamentary commander, resided at Friar's Place, according to tradition. The soldiers asked who the rector was and what were his religious opinions. According to the author of *Mercurius Rusticus*, the parishioners said

> he was a man who precisely observed the Canons of the Church … using all the Rites and Ceremonies of the Church established by Law. Some of the Red Coats replyed, Doth he so? We will teach him another lesson and make him leave those Popish superstitions, or he shall rue it.

The soldiers then went on the rampage.

> Soone after, they repaire to the Church at Acton, break open the doores by force, in the Chancell they find this inscription on the wall, This Chancell was repaired and beautified such a yeare by Daniel Featley … which they utterly defaced. Then laying hands on the Rayles, they dealt with them … and afterwards burnt them in the street, saying That if they had the Parson there, they would burne him with his Popish Trinkets.

The soldiers consumed all the food and wine in the rectory. The rector's barn and stables, the former full of corn, was burnt by the soldiers, possibly whilst drunk. Losses amounted to £211. Nationally, many other churches were attacked and their ornamentation (seen as crypto-Catholic) destroyed.

Featley's fate was little better. His attachment to the Prayer Book made him a marked man. He fled to Lambeth, his other parish, and soldiers confronted him there when he was conducting divine service. They threatened to chop him up because he allowed the Book of Common Prayer to be used in his churches. He managed to escape at the end of the service. Featley was voted a traitor and a spy by Parliament after he refused to sign the Covenant which declared that it was lawful to fight the King. He lost both his livings and was put under house arrest in London from 1642-4. His

health failing, he was moved to Chelsea and died there in 1645, being buried at Lambeth.

It might be thought that Featley was an arch-royalist to have so earned the wrath of the Puritan soldiery. In fact the reverse was true. He was a Puritan himself, a hater of Catholics and eager to argue with Charles I's right-hand man, William Laud, Archbishop of Canterbury. But he professed to be the King's friend as well as a moderate supporter of Parliament. It was probably his love of dispute and debate which caused him so much trouble, for these were dangerous luxuries in a time of civil strife.

It would seem that for much of the early 1640s troops were billeted on Acton; certainly from early August 1642. The King's headquarters in 1642-5 was at Oxford and therefore Parliament billeted troops on villages to the west of London. In 1644 it was announced that a troop of Captain John Marshall's cavalry was not to be billeted in Acton, perhaps a sign that the village was already too full of soldiers. In the following year, it was said there was money owed to the parishioners for feeding and housing the soldiers billeted upon them.

After the King's defeat at Naseby in 1645, there were three years of uneasy peace before war was renewed. In October 1648 it was rumoured there was a plan by Royalists to meet at Acton and Brentford, to the number of 500, to march on the capital and destroy their enemies there. General Fairfax quartered cavalry at both Acton and Brentford who were to watch for any plotters. By 13 November there had been no sign of anyone, and it was believed the presence of the soldiers had scotched the plot. They were then recalled.

Meanwhile, in 1643, another rector had been appointed to Acton, this time one rather more sympathetic to the Parliamentary regime, Philip Nye. At first he was among the moderate Parliamentarians, who wanted the King to share government with Parliament. Later he joined the radical Independents who aimed at complete Parliamentary supremacy. Nye was one of the commissioners chosen to propose conditions to the King when he was a prisoner at Carisbrooke Castle and he was given £500 for his services.

Nye had a long beard and a high opinion of himself. Like many previous rectors, he did not live in Acton but had a house in London and drove down to Acton in a coach with four horses in order to preach on Sundays. In 1650 his son assisted him and was being given half of the living's annual salary. According to Richard Baxter (of whom more anon), Nye was so unpopular locally that only two people took Holy Communion when he was rector, whereas previously there had been 200 communicants. Yet he did some good, restoring the rectory stables and barns damaged by his confederates in 1642.

After the battle of Worcester on 3 September 1651, where Charles II's army had been routed, 300 coaches came to 'a Green betwixt Acton and London' on 12 September to welcome Oliver Cromwell after his triumph. These coaches carried the Lord Mayor, his aldermen and councillors, MPs and others. The Trained Bands followed them on foot. Speeches were given, one by Nye. According to *Mercurius Politicus*, 'All the Fields were thronged with innumerable Flocks of People … all testified their Joy in his victorious return'.

In 1653 Nye became a member of the Committee of Triers, which was to vet any man who wished to become a clergyman. He ceased to be rector in 1654 and was replaced by Thomas Elsford in 1656. Elsford was referred to by John Perryn, the East Acton goldsmith, as being 'an orthodox and godly minister', though Elsford was probably not ordained! Certainly his name does not appear in the lists of Oxford and Cambridge graduates. Possibly he had been to one of the Scottish universities, as the newly installed vicar of Ealing had been.

It seems that a number of Parliamentary officers resided in Acton after the main phase of the war was over in 1645. The best known of these was General Philip Skippon. He lived in Acton House (rebuilt by Sir Henry Garraway, once Lord Mayor of London, in 1638), which was at the junction of Horn Lane and Churchfield Road, in the 1650s. His daughter was married in Acton in 1655 and his first wife died there in 1656. There is a plaque to her in the church. He was an officer in the Trained Bands and helped lead them at Turnham Green. Later he served at both battles of Newbury, being wounded in the second. Although one of the King's Judges, he did not take part in the trial. Skippon died in 1660 and his son sold the house in 1686. In 1653 there were also two colonels and four captains resident at Acton.

Another Parliamentarian who resided in Acton from 1651 was Lord Rous, Provost of Eton, whose wife Philippa died at Bank House, near St Mary's in 1657. There is a memorial plaque to her in the church. Rous, a staunch Puritan, had been ennobled by Cromwell and was Speaker of the Little Parliament in 1653. His funeral cortège in 1659 began at Bank House and travelled to Windsor, and his corpse was interred in Eton. Members of the Privy Council, naval and military officers were present.

After Cromwell's death in 1658 he was succeeded by his son Richard, who lacked his father's political skills. Two years later Charles II was restored to his birthright. Old scores began to be settled and others looked to gain redress for their wrongs. James Reade, who had been in the Tower of London for nearly three years, asked for his property in Acton, now in the possession of one Mr Deane, to be returned. Since neither appear in the Hearth Tax lists for Acton from 1664-74, the outcome of this matter is uncertain. John Davies of Acton, a suspected traitor, was sent to the Tower in 1662 for 'high crimes' and his large house (boasting ten hearths) was searched for weapons.

8 Francis Rous, Parliamentarian and Acton resident.

Yet he had probably been released by 1664 as his name is recorded as a property owner in the Hearth Tax assessment of that year.

Nye almost did not receive a royal pardon after 1660, and died in obscurity. Elsford was ejected from his living in 1661 and Dr Bruno Ryves, chaplain to both Charles I and Charles II, was rewarded for his loyalty and services as a propagandist by becoming rector of Acton, as well as being given a handful of other clerical appointments. In this period there were various attempts, by persons unknown, to rewrite recent history. This entry in the marriage register – 'Tuesday 5th April 1655, Richard Meredith, Esq., was married to Mrs Susannah Skippon, daughter to the Right Honourable Major General Skippon, by Sir John Thorogood, in a public congregation, Mr Philip Nye at the same time praying and teaching upon the occasion' – has 'Right Honourable' crossed out and 'traytor' inserted, and 'knave' was written above Sir John's name. Similarly, the titles were erased or cut out of the monument in the church to Lady Rous.

Ryves was largely, though not wholly, as we shall see, absentee rector of Acton. A curate, Solomon Saunders, looked after the parish from 1662. What little we know of him is from the pen of Richard Baxter, who described him as 'a dull weak fellow that spent most of his time in alehouses and read a few dry sentences to the people but once a day'. However, he was a regular attender at the vestry meetings (often held in the *George*) and the Visitation reports describe his work as being competent. Saunders may have matriculated at Exeter College in 1658 before graduating at Gloucester Hall in 1662. He was from humble origins, having been one of the servitors, the lowest class of scholars, at Oxford.

Perhaps Acton's most celebrated resident in this period was Richard Baxter (1615-91), a famous nonconformist preacher from Kidderminster, who had to live away from London because of the Five Mile Act, barring nonconformist preachers from being any nearer to a corporate town. He had been offered a bishopric, but left the Church of England in 1662 as he was unable to sign the new Act of Uniformity. He arrived in Acton on 14 July 1663 and lived with his wife, who was 30 years his junior, in a small house opposite the church door. His religious convictions were controversial; on one occasion, while preaching to friends (many of his congregation were probably from outside the parish) at home, there was a botched attempt to assassinate him. Later a lady asked if she could hear him preach and an appointment was arranged, but Baxter was warned that she plotted his death and so did not meet her again. Yet he continued to attend the parish church and encouraged the members of his conventicle to do so too. Baxter

9 Seventeenth-century house on Acton High Street, once (but not now) thought to be the dwelling of Richard Baxter.

lived in two houses whilst in Acton and wrote his autobiography there, which was published after his death.

Despite his alleged moderation, however, he fell out with Ryves. This seems to have been because Baxter called Ryves to his face 'a swearer, a curser, a railer'. Under such provocation, Ryves was fully justified in acting against him and Baxter was denounced, arrested and gaoled for holding public worship in his house. Baxter claimed that the whole parish was outraged over his treatment but, after he was discharged, he was forbidden to return to the county and his conventicle was dissolved. There were only two dissenting families in Acton at the beginning of the 18th century, their children being recorded in the baptism registers. There were also very few Acton Catholics, two

being recorded in the first decade of the new century.

The great plague of 1665-6 had a substantial impact in Acton. According to Baxter, its local effects began to be felt on 29 July 1665. Baxter fled to a friend's house in Buckinghamshire, leaving his family in Acton – hardly his finest hour. On his return home, he was surprised to find his wife and children still alive. He also noted that the churchyard was 'like a ploughed field with graves, and many of my neighbours dead'. The extent of the deaths in Acton is hard to measure, but was certainly severe. Unfortunately, the burial registers for 1665-6 do not specify causes of death and there were no burials recorded between 13 September 1665 and 6 May 1666. The record of marriages is also patchy and confused at this point. Presumably

Saunders, and/or the parish clerk, had fled the parish and so there was no one to read the services or keep records.

Some deductions can be made. In 1664 there were 24 burials; in 1667, 28. Yet in the first nine months of 1665, 50 were recorded – 19 in August and 17 in the first 13 days of September. We cannot ascertain the total number of deaths, but it would appear the numbers dying were large, being at least double (and probably far more than that) those in non-plague years. In 1664 the population was about 655; in 1670 it had fallen to 570. Perhaps nearly 100 people, almost a sixth of the population, had died during the plague. According to Baxter, it had ceased by 1 March 1666. The other great calamity of 1666 was also felt in Acton. Baxter noted that scorched leaves from books burnt in the Great Fire were carried by the wind to Acton, and even as far as Windsor.

Sir Matthew Hale (1609-76), a Lord Chief Justice of high integrity, lived in retirement in a house thought to be at the corner of Horn Lane and Churchfield Road. He was friendly with Baxter, first meeting him in church, and often listened to his preaching, to the disapproval of some, especially as he was a lawyer. In his will, Hale left Baxter his great Bible. Both men are commemorated in the carved heads by the west door of the church.

Anthony Saunder's rectorship (1677-1719) was less eventful but more constructive. He dealt with the problem of the church's physical condition. The altar rails, damaged in 1642, were at last replaced. The church was repaired and white-washed. This was the first time repair work had been carried out for many years and it cost £230. Charities were properly administered and a coal fund instituted: the parish would buy coal cheap in the summer and sell it to the poor at the same price in the winter, when coal was expensive. By now we have a clearer idea of what the parish officials did. One of their prime responsibilities

was to maintain the church. There are references to money spent on mending the clock, repairing the conduit, mending the altar rail and changing the bell ropes. They also helped the poor, whether the parish's own or those vagrants passing through. In 1687, 53 poor parishioners were given financial help totalling nearly £10 in all. Eleven years later, the 50 resident poor were given £7 10s. between them. In 1700 Richard Cooke was given two shillings because he was sick. After the end of the War of Spanish Succession, in 1713, discharged soldiers were given help as they returned to their homes; Acton helped 266 men in 1713-14, giving each two pence.

Nationally, the final decades of the 17th century were stormy as the Stuart monarchy tried to increase its authority, and some of the disputes were reflected locally. The climax came in 1688. James II was widely viewed as attempting to reintroduce Catholicism and subvert the Church of England. When a male heir was born on 10 June 1688 it seemed the Catholic succession was assured and Acton's bells rang to celebrate this event. Yet on 17 November that year, just after William of Orange's Protestant forces arrived in England to confront James II's army, Acton rang its bells to celebrate the anniversary of the accession of that icon of English Protestantism, Queen Elizabeth I, marking a clear shift in their allegiance. And when William had triumphed, his coronation day in 1689 was celebrated by ringing of bells, too. As we will see, two Actonians were involved, on different sides, in this conflict (and both lived, at different times, in the same house). Acton may have been a small village, but residents could not be unmindful of national events, and the church rang its bells to celebrate the King or Queen's birthday and the restoration of the monarchy on 29 May each year. When the town of Limerick fell to a siege, in 1691, the bells rang on that occasion, too.

There were a number of crimes in or near Acton in the 17th century, chiefly commonplace thefts and assaults. In 1613 William Crane, a yeoman, was charged with illegally shooting three pigeons. In the same year John Gates was cleared of concealing rogues in his barn at Gunnersbury. Likewise, William Freeman, a gentleman, assisted Tobias Wright, yeoman, in stealing three silver bowls and other silverware to the value of £14 from George Deacon. In 1614 John Dickson, yeoman, attacked Thomas Evington, gentleman. In 1615 Alice Raveninge of Long Crendon, Bucks, was robbed of various items of linen by William Griffen of Acton.

There was also an attack by Thomas Spurlinge, an Uxbridge butcher, on Mrs Ann Androwes in 1615. A year later, Edward Parker and Mary Plater, widow, kept a victualling house without a licence. In 1617 John Tracher the younger, a wheelwright, beat and wounded John Sheppard, his master. Tracher was sentenced to be whipped in public at Brentford on two market days, to be set in the stocks at Acton, and to seek pardon on bended knee on the church steps, and then spend one year in Newgate gaol. Tracher was also accused of getting Ann Roume with a child, which soon died. In the same year, Richard Northe was indicted of cattle theft. In 1650 Dorrell White, alias Thomas Brooke, alias Captain Smith, assaulted Mrs Jane Hampton and stole her rings worth £20 and four shillings. He was hanged. In 1664 Miss Joan Standberry of Hillingdon, riding through the parish and colliding with a cartload of beer, was thrown from the horse and died. The drayman was charged with murder, but acquitted.

Yet despite all this, from the early 17th century Acton was a fashionable place to live. It was becoming a retreat for the gentry at this time, as were many other places around London. John Hall, Shakespeare's son-in-law, had relatives and property in Acton. Actress Elizabeth Barry retired here in

1709 and died in 1713. Many used Acton as a retreat from London. Lady Conway was a summer resident in the 1630s. Lady Anne Southwell, a scholarly writer, rented premises in the Steyne and was buried in Acton in 1636. Lord Chief Justice Vaughan came to Acton in 1673 to live out his remaining years. Robert Sutton (c.1583-1633), a composer and musician at the courts of James I and Charles I, resided at Acton in the 1620s.

Berrymead's mansion had a number of distinguished residents, too. Sir John Trevor, a member of Cromwell's Council of State, built the house and lived there from 1660-73. From 1679-85 it was home to William Lloyd, Bishop of Norwich and Peterborough. He lost his bishopric in 1689 because he would not break his allegiance to James II after the King had been deposed following the Glorious Revolution of 1688. Ironically, the house then passed to a man of rather different political instincts, George Saville (1633-95), Marquis of Halifax from 1686-95, who entertained Queen Mary here in 1692. A leading privy councillor in the reign of Charles II, he later helped offer the crown to William and Mary. He is known as the 'Trimmer', but he was a moderate Anglican Tory, supporting the rights of the monarchy under Charles II whilst resisting the attempts of James II to advance the Catholic cause in England.

Why did these people come to live in Acton? It is probable that some, such as Hale, did so because they sought peace and quiet, especially those who had spent active lives. Some, such as William Lloyd, thought that a country house would be more suitable for bringing up a young family. In addition, mineral waters were found bubbling from Old Oak Common in the late 16th century and they were being publicised as early as 1612. Benjamin Allen, the writer, made the following remarks: 'a pint and a half of the [Acton] water yielded forty eight grains of salt, in which was six grains and a half of reddish Earth, which acid

Spirits wrought'. He also observed, 'the spring opens Northerly; is reputed to be one of the strongest purges about London … being more affected in grosser bodies'. Yet it was not to become fashionable until the following century.

A number of Acton charities began in the 17th century. The first was that of Thomas Thorney who left money in 1610 in order to provide the parish with a supply of clean water. The widow of Viscount Conway, who had been principal secretary to James I and Charles I, was an occasional resident of Acton during the summer months, and she left funds to found a parish charity. It was to help educate the poor and later funded scholarships to local schools. Several other charities were founded in Acton, which were later amalgamated in 1899 and are still being distributed. Often money was left to be invested and the income paid, each year, for food or clothing for the poor.

John Perryn, a London alderman, owned land in East Acton and on his death in 1657 left his estate to the Goldsmiths' Company, the income of which was to be used for charitable purposes, though it did not come into the Company's possession until 1682, after his widow died. It consisted of over 200 acres and property and ensured the Goldsmiths had a large share in East Acton for several centuries to come. Almshouses were first erected at the Steyne, by Charles Fox, in 1681. He sold his house and pound to the church-wardens for 30 shillings, in order that the property could be used for the benefit of the poor. They were rebuilt in 1887 as a Golden Jubilee memorial.

Acton's population in these centuries seems to have been reasonably static, except for the fall in 1665-6. There were 158 communicants in the parish in 1548, perhaps translating into a population of 790. In 1664 there were 131 households, which might equate to about 655 people. In 1674 it was 660. That there were more burials than baptisms was, explained the Rev. Lysons in his *History*, 'to be attributed to the number of strangers [i.e. non-parishioners] there interred'. An examination of the burial registers indicates that wandering vagrants who died in the parish were buried here, as were affluent shopkeepers and others from London. One reason for this was that the church-yards in London were becoming overcrowded.

St Mary's also witnessed a number of baptisms, marriages and burials of the great and good and the poor. Edward Lloyd, son of the bishop mentioned earlier, was baptised on 20 April 1680. Sir John Goodolfenne was buried one year earlier. Less grand were the burials of the anonymous vagrant poor, such as a vagabond found in Thomas Birch's stable in 1698 and a child found dead in a barn in 1710. William Aldridge, a wheelwright, was buried on 21 November 1698, allegedly at the age of 114. His grandson died in 1800, aged 92. Borough guides and other books regularly quoted Aldridge as evidence for the healthy air of Acton. Modern historians have questioned Aldridge's longevity, since there is no evidence for when he was born

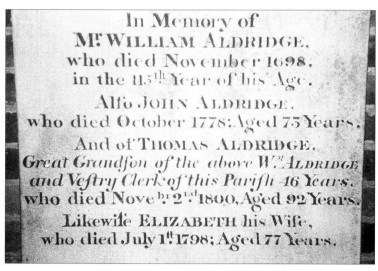

10 Memorial to William Aldridge, 1698.

and so no proof at all of his real age. It is probable that the reference in the parish register to his age was faked. Certainly the note of his age is in a different hand from that of the writer of his burial entry.

11 William Aldridge, alleged centenarian.

The number of houses in Acton was also fairly constant in the later 17th century. There were 131 occupied houses in 1664; 132 in 1674. Fifty of the larger ones were around Acton's centre. Nearly half (53) of all Acton's dwellings, though, were small, possessing only one hearth. One of the biggest houses was the mansion at East Acton, with 20 hearths in 1664. Like most villages, Acton possessed a small number of rich inhabitants, a larger number of the middling sort, and rather more, though not an overall majority, of the poor. It is not known whether there were any shops in Acton in this period. Farms would have sold their produce to the locals, who in any case would have been self-sufficient to a degree unimaginable today. There were also travelling salesmen, known as 'kidders'. These men were licensed to sell goods,

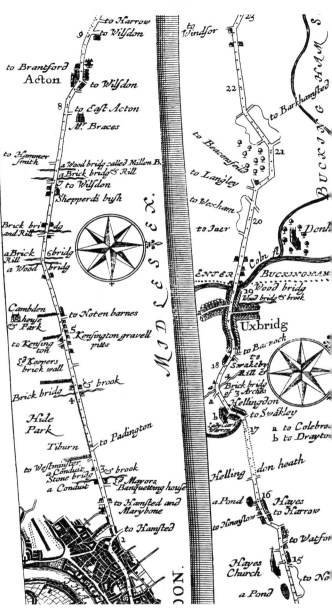

12 Part of Ogilby's map of the Oxford Road from London to Acton.

including livestock, either to the retail trade such as it was or direct to the customer. The Middlesex Quarter Sessions indicate that a number of Actonians were licensed to sell goods in such a fashion.

Parish registers between 1695-1705 show that there were a variety of different occupations among Actonians. The most common were labourers, as one might expect in a farming village. But there were shopkeepers and craftsmen, too, including coopers, butchers, glaziers, barbers, shoe makers, chandlers, bakers, carpenters, blacksmiths and even a collar maker. Transport was limited. Walking and riding would have been usual but traffic on the road through Acton appears to have been on the increase. Thomas Thorney provided water troughs, one for travellers, one for villagers, in 1610. Stage-coaches made their first appearance. Lord Ossultone found that he could travel between Uxbridge and London in two hours. Samuel Pepys recorded in his diary in the summer of 1666, 'then took coach and up and down in the country toward Acton'.

Towards the end of this period, Actonians had a rather bothersome problem on their hands for which they needed to petition Queen Anne. Heman Bryan had been executed in 1707 for burning down a house in central London. His body was taken to 'the west end of the town of Acton near the Gravel pits, between the road and the footpath' presumably to rot on a gibbet. Many considered this a problem: 'the smell of him is become very nauseous and offensive to your petitioners and all persons passing and repairing that road.' They wanted permission to take the body down and bury it. Alas, we do not know the outcome.

The middle of the 17th century had seen a number of dramatic and deadly events occur both in and near Acton. However, wounds were beginning to heal by the end of the century. Much had remained constant. Acton was still a small farming village. Above all it had survived the major crises of the centuries of upheaval.

III

Georgian and Regency Acton, 1714-1837

Acton enjoyed a rather less dramatic history under the Hanoverian monarchs. It remained an agricultural, rural village; although change was afoot, and perhaps at a faster rate than in the previous centuries. Population growth was more apparent; trade and commerce began to be of greater importance; Acton Wells rose and fell, and schools began to emerge, as did stronger signs of religious plurality. One unfortunate point about this century is that it seems to have unwittingly generated a number of oft-repeated legends. That they have been put right by other historians, namely Mr Rowland and the Harper Smiths, has had but minimal effect. There will now be another attempt to lay them to rest.

In Acton Park is the monument that once stood in the grounds of Derwentwater House. It reads as follows:

> This monument was designed as a memorial of James Radcliffe, Earl of Derwentwater, as one of the leaders of the [Jacobite] rebellion of 1715, who was taken prisoner at the battle of Preston, tried in Westminster Hall and beheaded on Tower Hill, February 24th, 1716. It was erected by Lady Derwentwater, in the grounds off the mansion in Horn Lane … at which house she was at the time residing.

James II had been exiled in 1688, but his supporters, known as Jacobites, endeavoured to restore him (and his successors) to the throne on several occasions. In 1715 there was a major rebellion to try to place his son on the throne, and one of the English leaders of this movement was the Northumbrian Earl of Derwentwater. Acton House was, reputedly, the residence of Lady Derwentwater and her children in 1716, when her husband was in the Tower awaiting execution for high treason. It has been alleged that the earl's headless body was borne through the gates in the grounds and thereafter the iron gates off Newburgh Road would never be reopened. Other tales allege that he is buried beneath the obelisk and his headless ghost walks. The truth is less romantic.

Derwentwater never came to Acton when alive and did not pass through it afterwards. His corpse rested in Dagenham after being taken from Tower Hill, and found its eventual resting place in Dilston, the family seat in Northumberland. Yet his wife did briefly reside here in 1720. The stories owe more to the romance which developed after Jacobitism ceased to be a realistic political creed and became a mania for some sentimentalists and amateur historians. Nicholas Selby was one of these. In 1804 he built a house on Horn Lane and called it Derwentwater House, to be demolished in the early 20th century. An obelisk was placed in the grounds to commemorate the earl, with the misleading inscription noted above.

Acton did have Jacobite links, however. The principal leader of the rebels in Scotland in 1715 was John Erskine, Earl of Mar, at one time Secretary of State for Scotland. On 20 July 1714, at St Mary's,

13 The Derwentwater Obelisk in Acton Park.

Acton, he married Lady Frances Pierrepoint, who had hitherto lived at her parents' home at Berrymead Priory, Acton. Mar led the rebellion in Scotland in the following year, which failed, mainly because of his inadequacy. However, unlike Derwentwater, he escaped with his life.

During the final attempt to restore the Stuarts in 1745, St Mary's rang its bells to celebrate both George II's birthday and the anniversary of his coronation. On the following year, the bells were rung on 9 October 'when the Duke came from Scotland'. The Duke of Cumberland, George II's second son, victor of the battle of Culloden, had returned to England in the summer after pacifying the Highlands, but the ninth of October was the day specified by the government to mark the thanksgiving for the defeat of the rebels. At Culloden a regiment of cavalry, formed by the Duke of Kingston, helped complete the rout of the rebel army. Kingston is said to have entertained the King at Berrymead Priory.

Fordhook, briefly home of Henry Fielding, the novelist, has often been claimed for the parish of Acton, but it is on the eastern end of Ealing, the rate books of the latter clearly listing it as a property within that parish. Likewise, David Garrick, the famous actor of the 18th-century London stage, did not reside in Acton, though a relation did. Nathan Garrick inherited Lichfield and Suffolk Houses, both of which stood on the High Street in 1779. They subsequently passed to his successors, one of whom was called Nathan David Garrick. These Garricks were the great man's nephews.

Crime was an occasional hazard. The most high profile case was when Princess Amelia's former tutor, Dr Bell, was held up by a highwayman in 1774 while travelling by coach on Gunnersbury

14 Berrymead Priory, c.*1802.*

Lane. Princess Amelia was a daughter of George II and used Gunnersbury House as her summer residence. Other thieves operated on the main road, one walking from London with an Acton man and robbing him as they arrived on the outskirts of the village.

Acton continued to be the residence of a number of noblemen and gentlemen. Foremost among these was perhaps Evelyn Pierrepoint, the 1st Duke of Kingston, who owned Berrymead Priory at the beginning of the 18th century. His most famous daughter, whose married name was Lady Mary Wortley Montagu and who resided in Acton prior to her marriage, was a great traveller, reader and letter writer, and conversed with intellectuals of the day, including Alexander Pope, who resided in Twickenham. She also advocated inoculation against smallpox. Berrymead Priory was rebuilt in about 1802 as a gothic mansion,

very similar to the nearby Twyford Abbey. Another great house was The Elms, built in 1735 by one James Cole. Sir Joseph Ayloffe, a Keeper of Records, was the first owner, but in 1749 it passed to Samuel Wegg, remaining in his family until 1842. The Weggs came to Acton in the middle of the century from Colchester. They were lawyers and were also noted for their charitable work.

Acton was also the home of a number of lesser gentry, clergy and lawyers. According to *Pigot's Directory* of 1826, 'the environs are embellished with a variety of neat and elegant mansions, the residences of persons of respectability'. There were 32 such persons in all, a large proportion of whom dwelt in East Acton. The latter was probably so favoured because of 'the beauty of the situation … the scenery being beautifully picturesque and rural'.

What put Acton on the map of the fashionable world in the 18th century was its springs. Near

East Acton were three wells of mineral water, springing out of a deep clay and famed for their medicinal value. They were first noted as early as 1612, but were first popular during Anne's reign, and even more so later in the century. The water was white and sweet and a little bitter and was sold in London. There was also an Assembly Room and race course, and the hamlets of Friar's Place and East Acton were packed with people of all ranks in the summer, the springs being open from March to October. The number of pubs increased from 13 in 1716 to 21 in 1752. One Brookes in 1763 described the waters thus: 'It is very clear and without smell. The taste is a little nauseous like a weak solution of Epsom salt. It will curdle with soup; and with salt of Tartar it produces a white grumous cloud.' Individuals could pay half a guinea and families a

15 The Elms, Acton Hill.

guinea to use the Assembly Rooms for consumption of the waters.

Decline had set in at least by 1776, as demand for the waters fell. As a contemporary writer noted,

16 Acton Wells, c.1800.

'The wells have long since lost their celebrity, fashion and novelty having given a preference to springs of the same nature at a greater distance from the metropolis.' Towards the end of the century, the wells became unfashionable and people went elsewhere. The Assembly Rooms were in ruins by 1795. The number of pubs also declined in number. Brewer, writing in 1816, was critical of visitors, dismissing those who indulged in a fashion of an earlier age as 'valetudinarian and idle inmates, allured with the hope of remedy or tempted by the love of dissipation'. The wells were not Acton's only claim to being a healthy place. Two women who died in the parish in the mid-18th century, were both allegedly centenarians. Furthermore, Dr Edward Cobden, rector of Acton from 1726-64 and a chaplain to George II, wrote of his parish's rural beauty:

> Give over all the busy care,
> of gain, and with despatch repair
> To Acton for untainted air.

Several new charities were founded in the parish, including those of Sarah and Ann Crayle.

The former, in 1730, left £300 to buy land in order that a sermon to her memory might be read and that money and bread might be distributed to the parish's poor. Twenty-nine years later, Ann gave £700 in bank stock to be spent on food and clothing for six men and six women. The poor, other than these dozen, were to receive coals. Edward Dickinson, in 1781, left strict instructions on the distribution of the income from the stock he left: the recipients had to be three poor couples who had been married in Acton in the last year and were also to be 'labouring, honest, industrious, and sober'. Finally, Mrs Rebecca Bulmer left £600 to charity in 1789. There was also 'Near East Acton … a fine range of almshouses'. These had been built by the Goldsmiths' Company in 1811 at the cost of £1,200. The buildings formed three sides of a quadrangle and comprised 'twenty uniform and commodious habitations'. They housed ten elderly men and ten aged women. Each received a pension and a 'moderate quantity' of coals in winter time.

Three of Acton's gentlemen who voted in the 1769 election (including Samuel Wegg, JP) cast their

17 Goldsmiths' Almshouses.

votes for the government's candidate, Colonel Luttrell. His opponent was self-proclaimed radical John Wilkes, who was not above using the London mob to assist his cause. Although Wilkes had the greatest number of votes, the government did not want him as an MP, and held a number of polls in order to obtain the result they wanted. Eventually they had to concede and Wilkes became MP for Middlesex, doubtless to the chagrin of the three Acton gentlemen. In 1802 Acton had an electorate of 50 but, of these, 22 were men living outside the parish who had property within it.

From the 1760s stage-coaches began to make short journeys from Acton to the City of London. One was the celebrated Acton Machine, which first made its appearance in 1764. The charge was one shilling and sixpence. It collected passengers from the *George and Dragon* pub each morning at nine and took them to the *Green Man and Still*, Oxford Street. It made the same journey at five o'clock. Return journeys were made from London at eleven and six. On Sundays one journey, beginning at Acton at nine in the morning, was made. By the 1830s, though, about thirty vehicles travelled through Acton into central London. These were not aimed at the poor (who could not have afforded the fare), nor the rich (who owned their own private carriages), but those of middling incomes who needed to transact business in London.

In order to finance the repair of the roads, which was increasingly important given the rise in traffic, the Uxbridge Turnpike Union was formed in 1714. This set up toll gates along the road to levy money from passengers. Foot travellers paid nothing, but horsemen paid a penny, a coach with two horses paid two pence and oxen cost ten pence per score. Acton's toll gate stood in what is now the Vale until the scheme ended in 1872. The other new mode of transport during the Hanoverian period was the canal. The Grand Junction Canal laid one of its branches towards Paddington along

18 Milestone in Acton.

the northern end of Acton's parish boundary in 1805. Although mainly aimed at cargo, it carried passengers from Paddington to Uxbridge in the 1820s. Coal was the chief 'import' while rubbish was loaded on the barges on to the return voyage. As part of the canal ran through the northern tip of Old Oak Common, the Company was obliged to compensate the parish financially.

We know, for the first time, what Acton's layout looked like, thanks to the map of the countryside around London designed by John Rocque in the early 1740s. The major portion of the village lay around the main road and the church. The two principal houses, Berrymead Priory and the Elms, stood, respectively, to the east and west of this collection of houses. There was also a mill not far to the north-west of the Elms. The other four settlements were more isolated. Although East Acton Lane connected East Acton with the main road, one had to walk across fields to reach Acton proper. Smaller still were the collections of houses around Friar's Place and Old Oak Common (one of the latter being Acton Wells) in the north of the parish. South of the main village were the few dwellings to the north of Acton Green, lying just north of the Brentford Road. Unsurprisingly, in such a rural district, fields predominated, comfortably separating Acton's built-up area from those of the neighbouring parishes of Ealing, Chiswick and Willesden.

One traditional annual event was the ceremony known as beating the bounds, when a group of parishioners would walk around the parish boundaries. In the years before detailed maps it was important to know where the boundaries were, but there was also a recreational aspect. In 1816 the parish spent just over £54 on the event, most of it at six public houses.

There are also contemporary descriptions of early 19th-century Acton. Brewer wrote in 1816 that Acton

> wears the appearance of a small and quiet country-town. The village is constructed on an unequal site, and contains a few substantial mansions; but the hand of improvement has not been generally busy in this neighbourhood, and the major part of the houses are beneath mediocrity of character.

East Acton had a rather more select air according to Brewer:

> This hamlet is scarcely one quarter of a mile from the high thoroughfare; yet as to acquirement of rural character, it would appear to be very far distant from any populous town. There are many respectable dwellings situated in this part of Acton.

One of the families living here in the 1730s even had a black servant.

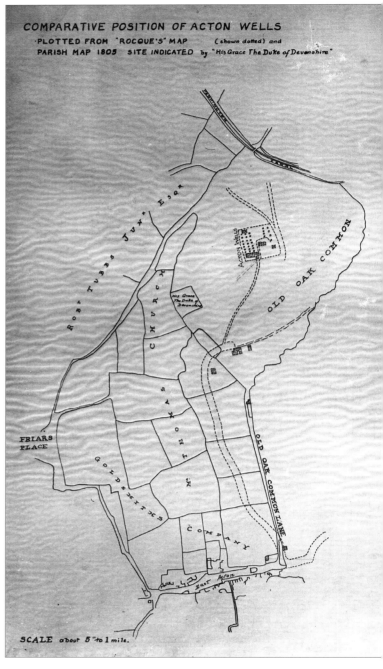

This was not an age of religious indifference, as it has been portrayed, and St Mary's received considerable attention. From 1701-86, £520 was spent on the church fabric. The old flint walls were

19 Maps showing Acton Wells and part of Rocque's map, showing Acton.

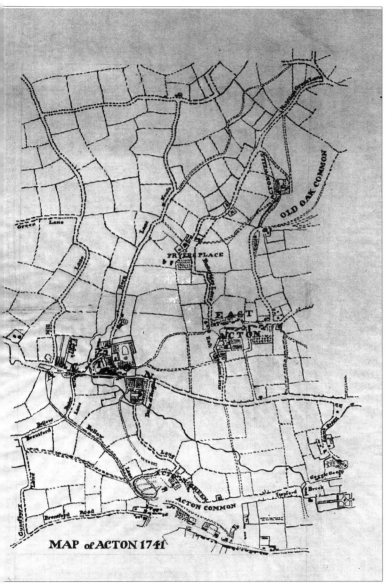

MAP of ACTON 1741

was repaired and painted, costing £135. Substantial work occurred between 1802-5, including the building of a gallery and a new pulpit. Such was the work carried out on the church in the late 18th and early 19th centuries, that between 1816-36 no repairs or other work was needed. Yet the church attracted unfavourable comment. The Bishop of London remarked that it was the ugliest in the diocese. Brewer thought it merely as dull as most in Middlesex, with 'little to interest the examiner'.

Acton's (joint) longest-serving rector was the Rev. William Antrobus, from 1797-1853. He was a powerful figure in the parish, and acquired 127 acres of land in Acton during his life. He was also very active in parish governance, helping deal with the cholera scare in the 1830s. He had galleries built in the church, which was becoming too small to fit all his parishioners inside, and was remembered by an old schoolboy for the length of his sermons, often lasting three quarters of an hour. Henry Mitchell, parish clerk, recounts the tale:

> The 'old schoolboy' recollected one of his texts 'Son of Man, eat that thou findest; eat this roll, so I opened my mouth, and he caused me to eat that roll'. He said, 'We boys wished he had eaten that sermon before he came'. The tuck shop was evidently a more pleasing remembrance than the Rector's long discourses.

After Antrobus' death, a road in Acton was named after him.

Most of Acton in this period was solidly Anglican. There was only one Acton Catholic in 1767 and none in 1790. Catholic worship became legal in 1791. Nicholas Selby of Acton House was a Catholic and a cottage on the estate served as a chapel for his co-religionists in

bricked over, the south porch and vestry were removed, and a large stove was installed in a specially built recess. A new vestry room was built by the south side of the tower. In 1766 the tower

20 Acton High Street, c.1799.

the early 19th century, mainly consisting of Selby's and Peter Kelly's (to whom Selby leased a house) families and servants. They were augmented by Irish workers from Turnham Green. Selby also sheltered French nuns who had escaped from the Terror in their own country in the 1790s.

Nonconformity was represented by a Congregationalist chapel on Acton Hill from 1817, though at first there were only about twelve worshippers. The Methodists met in a house at the junction of the Steyne and the High Street during the same period. Mrs Ann Carter's house in East Acton was used by nonconformists from East Acton and Hammersmith in the 1820s. Two more houses in the hamlet were registered for worship in the following decade.

There was very little schooling in Acton until the early 19th century. The Church, aided by charities and private subscriptions, played a large role in the provision of schooling for the poor. The National School, founded in 1816 after discussion in the vestry, was the principal establishment. Buildings near the church provided classrooms for 50 boys and 50 girls, who were taught by a salaried school mistress. It was paid for by wealthier local people.

There were a number of small private schools in Acton, which were mostly for boarders. Orger House, near the Steyne, was used for at least two schools: from 1804-12 for educating clergymen's sons, and from 1826 to the 1850s as a general boarding school for boys. Miss Frances Beechey

21 *View of Acton from the south-west. Note church and open countryside.*

22 *East Acton village, 1810.*

ran a girls' boarding school in the 1820s
and 1830s, later running a boys' school.
The old Assembly Rooms at Acton Wells
were also used as a private school. These
schools had relatively low numbers of
pupils: Miss Beechey's school had about
forty in 1832; the Orger House school
had eighty. By 1833, however, pupils of
fee-paying parents outnumbered those
at the National School by two to one.

Agriculture remained the predomi-
nant occupation of the men of the
parish, but it is only with the first national
census in 1801 that we have an idea of
the numbers of employed. Out of an
adult male population of perhaps about
400 (total parochial population 1,425),

23 St Mary's church, in the late 18th century.

215 were engaged in farming, although by 1831
this had fallen to 182. In 1816 Brewer wrote that
the land in Acton is 'chiefly used for agricultural
purposes'. On the Featherstonhaugh estate, to the
north and west of the parish, there were 740 acres
of land. This was divided, roughly evenly, between
arable and grass. The latter was useful for the
production of hay to feed the large numbers of
horses which worked in London. More of the
arable land was turned over to hay from 1800.

24 Acton Rectory.

What arable there was, was divided into two large farms which grew wheat, beans, oats, peas, potatoes and clover in the first decade of the 19th century.

There was relatively little industry. In 1801 there were 141 people involved in trade, crafts and manufacturing, falling to 128 thirty years later. These people were employed in small-scale enterprises. There was a little brickworks near Mason's Green in 1799, but this was not fully exploited until much later in the 19th century. There was a tanyard and mill house in the Steyne. This included a mill yard in 1728 and was later known as the Steyne Mills. In 1832 it made Lapland rugs and footwear, scouring blankets and counterpanes. The number of shops and traders in the village had grown. In 1826 there were 64 in total. Many were commonplace providers: grocers, bakers, butchers, fishmongers and a bootmaker; others were suited to the needs of farming, such as John Clifton, corn dealer, Christopher Day, saddler and Joseph Smith, who was a blacksmith and farrier. There were also a number of shops selling specialist goods, including a toy dealer, a perfumer and a watch and clock maker, and there was even an agent for the Norwich Union fire insurance company. There was also a regular postal service for both Acton and East Acton, with letters collected in the morning and afternoon and arriving in the evening. The grocery shops in both places acted as post offices.

Population growth was rather steadier. In the middle of the 18th century, there was an estimated population of 800. In 1801 there were 1,425 residents, rising to 2,453 in 1831. The number of inhabited residences also rose from 241 in 1801 to 426 in 1831.

Local government was still in the hands of the vestry. Meetings were held in the church before adjourning to a public house. There were several meetings each year, the most important being those which elected the officers (held at Easter) and those which decided upon the rates in order to repair the church and make provision for the poor. Eighteenth-century rates were usually at three pence or four pence in the pound, but they rose sharply towards the end of the century. In 1801 they were 20 pence in the pound, but this was due in part to the increase in poverty owing to wartime conditions. Cheap food was provided for the poor, as well as cash payments. Yet, by 1828, Acton was not considered to be a poor parish, since only three able-bodied men were unemployed. New officials were appointed in addition to the customary ones, pointing to an increase in the amount of work which was necessary. Inspectors of weights and measures were appointed in 1798, and a beadle in 1800.

Children of poor parishioners were occasionally apprenticed to learn a useful trade and to keep the rates down, including 19 between 1760-80. Their masters were tradesmen or craftsmen living in the parish or in nearby parishes. All but two of

25 Acton village pump.

those apprenticed in these 20 years were boys. Some apprenticeships were paid for by one of the Acton charities.

National events were celebrated by the ringing of the church bells. These included victories in the Seven Years War against France, the taking of Pondicherry in India or the successes enjoyed by Prince Ferdinand's Anglo-German army on the continent in 1761. Yet, oddly enough, there seem to have been no recorded celebrations of Trafalgar or Waterloo. As ever, royal events and anniversaries were marked. In 1810 bells rang for King George III's Jubilee, as he became the first monarch to reign over Britain for 50 years.

During the Napoleonic Wars, volunteers were raised in Acton, as elsewhere, against the possibility that Napoleon might try to invade. John Delamain

of East Acton wrote, on 23 October 1803, 'I have only to add that Acton has raised a company of volunteers which are attached to the Ealing and Brentford corps. They received their colours last Thursday, which made a fine holiday for the surrounding country.' A subscription was opened in the parish to raise funds to pay for the men's uniforms and to compensate the poorer volunteers for the loss of their time. If Britain were invaded, the men were to act in conjunction with other units in order to repel the foe. This contingency never arose as Britain remained in control of the Channel. A rather more active soldier was Captain William Hart of the 79th Regiment of Foot. He was killed in 1815 and buried at St Mary's.

Life on the 'Home Front' during the long wars with France was difficult for some. Food shortages

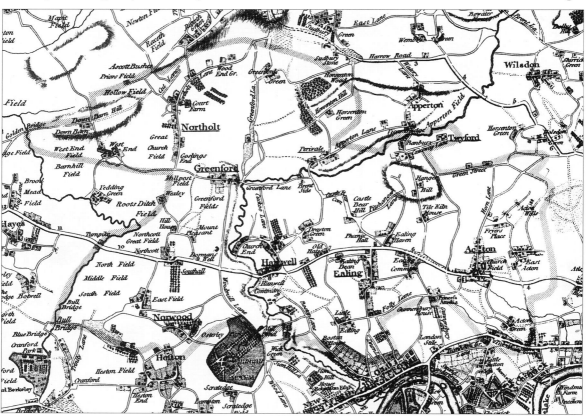

26 Cary's Map of Middlesex, 1786.

27 *Acton Windmill*, c.*1800*.

hit the poor hardest. In 1800 the wealthy were asked to restrain from over-eating, which would have meant that prices could rise and the poor would be worse off. In the winter, meat, bread and coals were to be supplied to the poor at reduced prices. Clothing was given to the elderly poor, and weekly cash allowances were available. Payments were given to the families of men serving in the militia to stop them becoming needy. When the wars were over, the parish petitioned the government about the rises in taxation 'which they had hitherto sustained without complaint'. In particular, they objected to the 'partial, oppressive and inquisitorial' Income Tax.

Eighteenth-century Acton was still a rural village in which the seats of the gentry and the church were dominant. Yet a number of changes were occurring. There was an increase in traffic through the parish, the beginnings of religious diversity, the advent of schools and an increasing number of shops and potential customers. None of these developments was by itself dramatic. Many followed existing national and local trends, but they did serve as pointers towards the future.

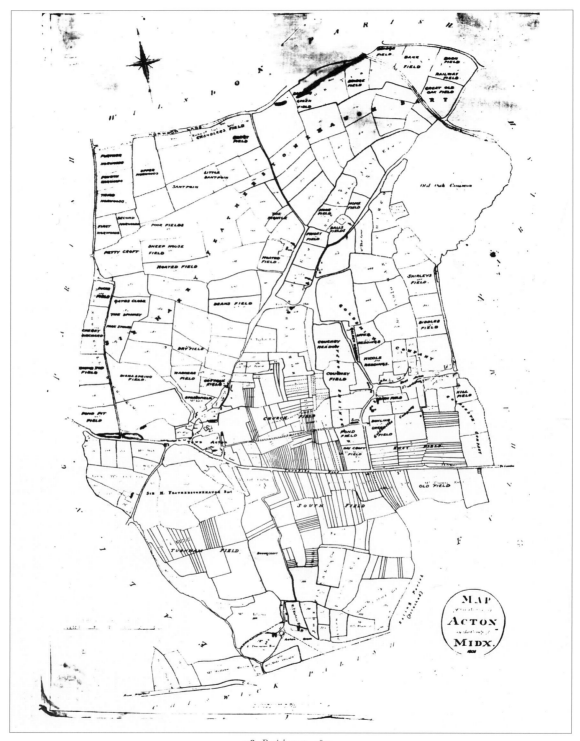

28 Parish map, 1805.

IV

Victorian Acton, 1837-1901

Acton was transformed forever in the late 19th century. However, Henry Mitchell, for many years parish clerk at St Mary's, observed that, 'During the years 1840 and 1850, the Parish remained almost the same as it had been for many years.' Population stood at 2,665 in 1841. *Pigot's Directory* for 1839 remarked, 'This is an agricultural parish … the village itself, which consists of one long street, has little to boast in the way of appearance.' There were a number of gentlemen's houses and a few shopkeepers, but that was all. Most of the latter were specialists: butchers, carpenters, bakers, dressmakers. The agricultural nature of the parish is suggested by the fact that there were three black-

smiths, a corn dealer, three cowkeepers, a wheelwright and two stablekeepers. In 1863 Acton was described as 'this quiet village', and four years later there was a reference to 'a rural place like Acton'. The majority of residents in the early 1860s lived close to the High Street and many lived in the Steyne, just north of the main road. Elsewhere in the parish there were open fields. Horn Lane, leading northwards from the High Street, was tree-lined and bordered by open fields, with only a few large private houses. By 1901, however, Acton had been transformed into a rapidly expanding suburb.

Mitchell refers to two ancient pastimes which still existed in early Victorian Acton. In the early

29 Shalimar, Horn Lane, c.1840s.

to mid-19th century there were two clubs made up of 'the labouring men of the village', who paraded around the parish, eating and drinking, every Whit-Monday. The clubs were the Ancient Britons, whose base was the *George Inn*, and the Young Britons, based at the *King's Head*. Blue flags and gold lettering adorned the windows of their favoured public houses all day. After eating, they visited parts of the parish, flags flying and bands playing. At Friar's Place Farm they were given home-brewed ale, before returning to their respective headquarters, 'some very tired'. Another popular entertainment was provided by the mummers, who dressed up in ribbons and paper and provided entertainment for themselves and onlookers in the

30 St Mary's church, c.1840s.

month before Christmas. The men would perform in the village and usually enjoyed a large audience. The roles included 'Molly', who used a broom to sweep the way, and 'King George', who kills the 'Turk' in battle. The latter is then brought back to life by the 'Doctor' giving him a large pill. There was also singing. Mr Pritchard, the builder and undertaker in the High Street, rewarded the performers with home-brewed ale.

In 1840 there were a number of schools in the parish. One was a Dame School kept by Mrs Preston. Henry Mitchell, who attended the school for a time, recalled the punishments in store for any miscreants:

> This school possessed a Fool's Cap, to be worn by naughty children, a high stool being brought from the hairdresser's shop on which to stand the culprit, so that he might be more easily seen than on a school form. I was once punished in this way, but I hardly need add that it was unjustly, for I was innocent. Another threatened punishment was to be put into the cellar where there was a 'tiger'. I do not think, however, that this threat was ever carried out.

Thomas Ives ran a stage-coach company which plied the main road between Ealing and the City of London. From Acton to the Bank of England the fare was one shilling and six pence; the fare to Regent Circus was one shilling. Later these fares were reduced. Not many in Acton used this form of transport, however. According to Mitchell, 'A few resident gentlemen went daily to Town and returned at 5pm'. There was another omnibus service which plied these routes, too, but both were slow, the complete journey taking one and a half hours at best.

Until 1861 Acton's population growth was modest. During the next two decades it multiplied by over five, from 3,151 to 17,126, and continued to grow, though at a slower rate, for the rest of the century, reaching 37,703 by 1901. Perceval Joliffe, a resident, described the changes in Acton in his lifetime:

> It would be a big undertaking to trace, in minute particular, the enormous growth of the town from the early [eighteen] seventies ... One by one its picturesque residential estates disappeared, the land was partitioned into small plots, and covered, in quick succession, with dwellings, which for the most part, house a wage earning

population. Nowhere has this great change been more apparent than in South Acton.

The event which was to change Acton forever was the Enclosure Award of 1859. It led to the disappearance of the common land throughout the parish. The British Land Company acquired fields in the south and began building small houses upon them, which led to thousands of people from all over the British Isles flocking to live there. Another important factor was Acton's proximity to London, which grew in the 19th century at a rate which it was never to do so again. From 1889 Acton was just outside the western boundary of the newly formed London County Council. It was described in an 1894 directory as being 'a metro-

politan suburban parish'. James Thorne, writing in 1876, concluded that Acton, 'never very interesting, has been rendered less so by building operations', adding that, 'On the west are some pretty lanes'.

One development which encouraged and enabled Acton's rapid expansion in the late 19th century was the railways. The Great Western Railway Company line westwards from Paddington had been in service as early as 1838, but the first station west of the capital had been in Ealing. It was easier for Actonians to use road transport if they wished, or needed, to travel to London. They could see trains steaming through the parish, but could not utilise them. But by the late 19th century they were spoilt for choice, Acton having the most

31 Traction engine at East Acton, c.1850.

stations and halts in any parish outside central London. The North and South Western Junction Railway was the first to build a station within Acton, in 1853 (it was later called Acton Central). By 1869 their line travelled south to Richmond and Brentford (via South Acton Station from 1880), and north-east to London. It allowed passengers to travel to Broad Street in the City of London in only half an hour, and so may have encouraged clerks and other similar workers to reside in Acton. A station was built on the Great Western line (later known as Acton Main Line) in 1868. The underground railways also pushed out their Metropolitan and District Lines through the parish in 1879, with stops at Mill Hill Park (now Acton Town) and Acton Green (now Chiswick Park). As well as those railways which were built, there were plans for another which was not. The Latimer Road and Acton Railway was envisaged as running south of the GWR line, towards Shepherd's Bush, but work on it was abandoned by 1900.

The roads in Acton also became vastly more busy. Horse buses plied the roads. A fleet of Bayswater buses went from Hanwell to the City, collecting passengers en route. A small operator ran buses between the railway stations in Ealing and Acton, and the London General Omnibus Company would stop in Acton on the way to London at regular intervals; in 1900, this was every fifteen minutes if they ran to schedule. Another form of transport first seen in Acton in the late 19th century was the trams. At first these were horse-drawn conveyances, although they travelled on rails embedded in the road. The Southall, Ealing and Shepherd's Bush Tramways Company opened the first part of what was intended to be a long tramway in 1874. However, it only extended from Shepherd's Bush as far as *The Askew Arms* in Acton, and the company went bankrupt and services ceased in the following year. This unhappy experience did not blunt the enthusiasm of others,

though. The tramway was extended to Priory Road in 1878, and by 1891 yet another company had taken over the enterprise, with ambitious plans to extend the line, this time limiting the route to Hanwell, and aiming to electrify it.

It was not until the London United Electric Tramways Company came into being that these plans were finally realised. By 1895 the line was yet again extended through Acton, inching its way westwards as far as Acton Hill, where a depot was established. Yet it was not until several years had passed that the ambition to run a tramway as far west as Southall was realised. In part this was because of the attitude of Ealing Council, who objected to the tramways running through their parish.

The motor car was first seen on the Uxbridge Road in 1899. At first it was objected that this was merely a dangerous plaything of young men who would hire a car at the weekend and drive at high speed. The local newspaper suggested that if a figure of authority were killed, the mind of the legislature would be exercised in restricting these dangerous vehicles. Their danger, of course, came as much from their rarity as from their speed.

Although some alterations were made to St Mary's church in the late 1830s, the most substantial change to the fabric came in 1865-6. The whole building, save the tower, was demolished and a new edifice constructed because the church was far too small to accommodate the increasing numbers. It cost £8,000, which was raised from subscriptions among the parishioners. Many of those who gave large sums towards the work had stained glass windows to the memory of themselves and their families. The church was consecrated on 16 May 1866 by the Bishop of Oxford, Samuel Wilberforce, yet the building was not finally completed until 1875-6, when it was decided to build a new tower. The Ouvry family of East Acton paid nearly £3,000 for this to be accomplished.

32 St Mary's church, 1897.

One of the parish's secular duties was the distribution of income from the parochial charities, the latter being added to in the 19th century. In the year 1854-5, this sum amounted to £237. It went to provide food, clothing, shoes, blankets and coals to a number of deserving families in the parish. Two local lads were apprenticed and payment made towards their costs. Yet the parish was becoming of less and less significance as a unit of local government. Its Poor Law functions were hived off to the Brentford Union in the 1830s, and after 1866 its remaining secular duties were taken over by Acton Local Board. Yet the vestry carried on its work of meeting, appointing officers and levying poor rates until the end of the century.

There was a vast expansion in church building in these years. Some denominations just had temporary structures for the faithful; more permanent buildings in which worship could be conducted were needed. South Acton was blessed by two new Anglican churches. Firstly there was All Saints in 1872, on Bollo Bridge Road, and in 1888 there was St Albans on Acton Green. St Dunstan's in Friar's Place Lane served East Acton from 1879. Elsewhere there was St Andrew's in Salisbury Street, from 1892, St Barnabas' in the Vale, from 1890, and St Luke's in Old Oak Lane, in 1895. St Andrew's and St Barnabas' were chapels of ease to St Mary's and St Dunstan's respectively.

The Catholics did not have a permanent place in which to worship in Acton in this period, though a resident priest was appointed to the parish in about 1878. He preached in a house in Shakespeare Road before being presented with an iron chapel in Strafford Road. Nonconformity was better established. The first Baptist chapel was in Church

Road from 1865, and in 1896 a chapel was established in South Acton. The Congregationalists, worshipping in Acton from 1817, moved to a chapel in Churchfield Road in 1871. The Methodists' headquarters was in the Steyne from 1845, but they relocated to premises in Gunnersbury Lane in 1858.

The increase in population and the Forster Education Act in 1870, which stated that where provision for elementary education was lacking the state should step in and provide, meant that something had to be done locally – and it was. Six denominational schools, National Schools for Anglicans, Wesleyan schools and a Catholic school, were all established by the 1840s-60s. More were

still needed and Acton School Board was founded in 1875 to deal with this issue. It was dogged with controversies, chief among which was the religious issue. Nonconformists objected to having to pay from the rates for the National Schools. A compromise was reached whereby schools could give what religious instruction they wished in the first three quarters of an hour of the school day, but thereafter the Board's authority held sway.

The School Board also built its own schools, known as Board Schools, which were to be non-sectarian as regards religious education. The first was built for infants on Osborne Road in 1880. The Priory Schools in Acton Lane, built in 1882 and extended in 1896, catered for both boys and

33 St Dunstan's church, East Acton.

34 St Alban's church, Acton Green.

35 The Rev. George Manbey, Vicar of St Alban's, 1892.

girls. Some of the denominational schools were converted into Board Schools, including the Wesleyan School in 1895. There was little scope for higher education, except what was provided by the Acton and Chiswick Polytechnic, established by the Middlesex County Council in 1899 in order that technical subjects, such as construction, architecture and millinery, could be taught.

A number of private schools, mostly small and short-lived, existed in Acton at this period. There were a dozen in 1873 and 15 in 1890, nine of the latter being for girls. The nuns at Berrymead Priory ran a Catholic boarding school there from 1842 until their departure in 1850. One of the longest survivals was Acton Collegiate Day School, which was founded in 1864. It offered mathematics, modern languages, science and training for university entrance. A school with a similar curriculum was Acton Commercial School, founded in 1896 on premises in the High Street. Leith House in Burlington Gardens was a girls' day and boarding school from 1890, designed to fit girls to pass entrance examinations.

36 All Saints' church, 1901.

By 1894 most of that part of Acton to the east of Gunnersbury Lane and west of the North and South Western Junction Railway was completely built upon and was largely residential. As a result, few of the orchards in south-east Acton to the west of Acton Green survived. To the north of the High Street, housing had reached as far as the Great Western Railway. Only the fringes of the parish had yet to be built over. East Acton was still a separate entity from Acton proper, surrounded as it was by allotments and sports fields, but buildings were being erected to the north of Acton Park, and its days were clearly numbered.

Acton's housing varied. Most of the land to the south of the High Street had, by the 1890s, become full of terraced housing for the working classes. Much of the rapid building at the end of the 19th century led to parts of the parish being 'overstocked with houses, built rather with a view to smallness of cost, than to the attractiveness and conveniences of the dwellings', according to contemporary historian William King Baker. He thought that the houses between Gunnersbury Lane and the border with Ealing were rather better, being 'filled up with a good type of medium size houses'. This was where many professional men lived. Apparently, Twyford Avenue was favoured by several local councillors as a dwelling place.

Yet some of these new (and old) houses were of poor quality and there were complaints of overcrowding. In 1899 it was discovered there were 18 people living in one basement flat, for example. Housing in the Steyne was also condemned for being as overcrowded and unhealthy as any slum in central London. There were calls that Acton Urban District Council should use powers granted to it by the Housing Act of 1890 to alleviate the problem, but little was done in the short term.

The pace of building came under fire from the Acton Ratepayers' Association, who in 1866 stated that they 'were not opposed to the Acton Local Board but opposed to the destruction of those rural features which were the real charm of Acton – the chief inducement of those working in London to come and live here'. Older buildings, such as a house

37 Staff and pupils of Gunnersbury Lane School, c.1895.

38 Apsley Terrace.

39 *Longfields Lane, 1890s.*

40 *East Row, The Steyne,* c.*1890s.*

41 East Acton village in the late 19th century.

where Richard Baxter was alleged to have lived on the High Street in the 1660s, were demolished (in about 1901 in the case of Baxter's house), as they were becoming increasingly decrepit.

The transformation from a village to a town required the construction of a number of public works. These were undertaken mostly by the Acton Local Board, which was the font of local government, replacing the centuries-old vestry. It was founded in 1866 and consisted of 12 (later 15) members, all men of local standing and property owners similar in status to those who had made up the vestry. They were chosen by election, but voting was limited to property owners. The Board employed a staff of qualified professionals and was replaced in 1894 by an Urban District Council. The Board received a great deal of criticism in the

local press, especially over allegations that it acted unfairly against small builders and that it built sewers to benefit those in Horn Lane rather than elsewhere.

One of the Local Board's first decisions concerned the issue of fire prevention. Steyne Mills burnt to the ground in the same year as the Board's formation and it was thought that Acton should have a fire brigade to prevent, or at least alleviate, this form of catastrophe. The brigade was formed in 1868 and, though the manual fire engine and appliances were provided by the Board, the men were volunteers. They were soon in action. Henry Collier's mushroom beds were alight in 1868, when it took the firemen 16 minutes to assemble. However, local wags stated that the fire engine was merely 'a plaything for a lot of young men in

42 Design for Acton Library, 1900.

the town'. A permanent fire station to house the steam engine was completed in 1899.

Perhaps the most important of the Board's other achievements was the creation of a proper drainage system in 1884-8. In the 1870s, wells, water pumps and even ponds were used for drinking water by the poor, even though a report in 1876 claimed most should be condemned. Their replacement cost a colossal £85,000. It was no surprise that the Ratepayers' Association said the sewers should be paid for not out of the rates but by those they directly benefited. By 1893 most of Acton received piped water from the Grand Junction Canal system, via the Kew Works. Another key improvement was the paving and kerbing of the major streets in Acton in the 1870s.

Some households and St Mary's church had gas lighting by the early 1850s. In 1859 it was suggested that gas lighting on the principal streets should be provided by Brentford Gas Company. Due to concerns over costs, it was not until 1863 that this came about. During the debate, one suggestion made was that gas should not be supplied on nights when moonlight was sufficient! Gas lit more of Acton's streets in the later 1860s and 1870s. Despite the competition from electricity in the 1900s, gas lighting remained commonplace throughout Acton until the 1930s.

The creation of a public library was first discussed in 1887 (four years after neighbour Ealing already possessed one). There had been little need earlier, as the Acton Literary Institute possessed books parishioners could borrow; it was flooded in 1880. Yet the library was opposed by the Ratepayers' Association, ever eager to save money, and in a referendum the idea was defeated. In 1898 it resurfaced, this time successfully. Passmore Edwards, a well-known benefactor to libraries throughout the country, donated £4,000 to help with the cost. It was opened by Joseph Choate, the American Ambassador, in January 1900 and was an instant success. Nearly 20,000 books were issued in the first two months of opening and over 1,000 people visited on each weekday.

Another of the council's major achievements in this period was the creation of Acton's first park, though this took seven years from its inception to its opening. Land was eventually purchased to the north of Acton High Street from the Goldsmiths' Company and from a private developer,

and the park was landscaped with mounds and valleys, rustic bridges and an oak bandstand. It covered 25 acres and was opened by Lady Hamilton, wife of one of Middlesex's MPs, in June 1889.

In 1801 there had been just nine public houses; by 1873 there were 19, plus 24 beer retailers (off-licences). There was briefly a biergarten in the 1870s, run by the German Club in London, on the site of the old wells on Old Oak Common. South Acton Working Men's Club was formed in 1872, but attracted criticism in the local press in 1901 when one man died there from over-indulgence in drink. More soberly, there was the Acton Coffee Public House Company, supported by the churches, which offered a social environment without any alcohol. Those seeking intellectual improvement might frequent the Acton Literary Institution between 1868-89, with its readings from

43 Acton Park, c.1890s.

44 Middlesex Yeomanry, South Acton, c.1890.

Dickens and its circulating library. The more athletic might play golf. An 18-hole course was opened to the north of East Acton in 1896. True to the spirit of the age, both ladies and gentlemen could exhibit their sporting prowess, but each sex had its own club house. Acton Amateur Cricket Club was formed in 1867, and a year later a company of rifle volunteers was formed, which held rifle shooting competitions, drills and social evenings. At the new lecture hall there was a negro concert in 1867. The Philanthropic Society, formed in 1870, held concerts and other entertainments to provide money for fuel and other essentials for the poor. Local political organisations, by the 1890s, included two Liberal and three Conservative clubs.

Acton's first local newspaper, *The Acton Press*, appeared in the 1860s but soon sank beneath the waves, to be briefly resuscitated between 1898-1900. The more permanent local organ was the weekly *The Acton Gazette*, which began life in 1871. By 1880 it included Parliamentary, City and world news, and had expanded to eight pages.

Whereas Acton had been known for its wells in the 18th, it became known for its laundries in the later 19th century. It acquired the nickname

45 The Bull's Head *and Laundries, East Acton, 1880s.*

46 Laundry workers' outing, c.1890.

'Soap Sud Island' as large numbers of them began to sprout up there. By 1873 there were about sixty, mostly hand laundries on the Mill Hill estate. Just over twenty years later there were at least 212. This compares, in 1895, with 10 laundries in Chiswick

47 Mr Charles Gee, laundry owner, 1890s.

48 Thistle Laundry, c.1890

and 24 in Ealing, Hanwell and Brentford. In 1901 just over 3,000 people were employed in the laundry trade, mostly women. Not all were small operations; Rush and Co. ran a large steam laundry from 1873 in the Steyne. The reason for the industry seems partly to have been that most of the men who rented the houses in South Acton were labourers and, in order to increase the family income, their wives took in laundry. Some of these houses were even built with special laundry facilities. Also, at the same time as these small houses in south Acton were being rented, there was a boom for rather larger housing in Acton, Chiswick and Ealing. Together with rich households in Notting Hill and Kensington, they generated the demand for laundry services which the poorer families were all too happy to meet.

Acton had a number of other industries in this period, though relatively few compared with what was to transpire in the next century. The major industry, apart from the laundries, was the brick fields. These had been known about since 1799, but were not properly exploited until about 1868. After receiving permission from the Charity Commissioners, the Goldsmiths' Company, as a major landowner in the parish, drew up agreements with a number of brick companies from that date until 1901, and work began in earnest. Indeed, from 1878-1904, between nine and twelve million bricks were made each year in Acton. Many of these bricks were used in local housing and can be seen in properties in Shaa, Perryn and Churchfield Roads, for example. Other industries grew up around the canal in the north of the parish, where

49 *James Omans, brickfield owner,* c.*1890.*

50 *Ruckholt Farm,* c.*1870.*

transport links with London were advantageous (the Willesden Railway Junction was also nearby). There was a Naphtha works there from 1868 to about 1890, which was replaced by saw mills. Waterproof paper was pioneered in a factory nearby from 1868.

Agricultural employment fell as the fields began to disappear beneath housing. In 1880 there had been 412 acres under plough; by 1890 this had fallen to 137. From 1870 to 1890 the number of cows dropped from 253 to about a hundred. There were 558 pigs in 1870, but only 322 in 1900. The corn mill near East Acton was demolished in the 1870s. But it is not a simple story of wholesale decline. The amount of land used to grow hay rose from 916 acres in 1870 to 1,211 in 1890, and market gardens developed in the far south of the parish, near Turnham Green. By 1890 almost 130 acres were used as market gardens and orchards.

Queen Victoria passed through Acton in the first year of her reign. Mary North wrote on 25 August 1837, 'We saw an open carriage and

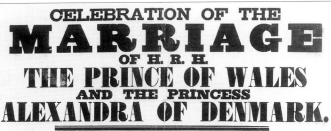

CELEBRATION OF THE

MARRIAGE

OF H. R. H.

THE PRINCE OF WALES

AND THE PRINCESS

ALEXANDRA OF DENMARK.

IT IS PROPOSED TO GIVE A PUBLIC

DINNER

to the Working Classes of Acton, and TEA to
their Children, at the National School Rooms.
For this object a Subscription is proposed, to
which your contribution is requested.

TREASURER,
THE REV. EDWARD PARRY, *Rector.*
COMMITTEE,

The Rev. J. N. OUVRY NORTH,	GEORGE PRICE, Esq.
FRANCIS HAMILTON, Esq.	JOHN WILLIAMSON, Esq.
G. STANLEY HINCHLIFF, Esq.	T. WOODHOUSE, Esq.
H. B. LINGHAM, Esq.	S. WRIGHT, Esq.

51 Advertisement of public dinner to celebrate the royal wedding of 1863.

52 (right) Acton Cottage Hospital, c.1900.

four with outriders coming into the village [East Acton]. We knew immediately it was our young Queen. The gentlemen took off their hats and she bowed most graciously. She went up to the common and we waited her return. All the village went out to see her; she looked very well.' In 1863 her son's wedding was celebrated. A band played English and Danish national anthems, and children sang 'God Bless the Prince of Wales'. The Golden (1887) and Diamond (1897) Jubilees of the Queen were celebrated locally as they were elsewhere. There were both festivities and more lasting commemorations. These included council offices being illuminated with the royal crown, special sermons in church, a dinner for the aged poor and treats for school children. Almshouses were rebuilt in the Steyne in 1887-8 and a recreation ground was proposed to mark the event. The Cottage Hospital on Gunnersbury Lane was built to mark 60 years of the Queen's reign in 1897-8.

Acton's society was mixed. In South Acton there was a working-class population of 15,000, but to its east, overlapping the parish boundary of Chiswick, was the rather better-off Bedford Park. Springing up in the 1870s and 1880s, this housing estate was home to 'some of the most popular actors and actresses of our modern [Victorian] stage, besides many people famous in the world of art and literature'. One such was W.B. Yeats, then a young journalist living with his affluent family, but later to become Ireland's greatest poet. Bedford Park was known as the first garden suburb in England, preceding Brentham and Letchworth by several decades. Jonathan Carr, a cultured social reformer, was its founder in 1875. It boasted wide roads, tree-lined streets, 'Queen Anne' houses, many designed by Norman Shaw, art studios and tennis courts. Many of the streets were named after events and people of Queen Anne's reign (1702-14), such as Blenheim Road or Newton Grove.

Yeats recalled his time there as a child:

> We went to live in a house like those in the pictures and even met people dressed like people in the story books. The streets were not straight and dull like those at north end, but wound about where there was a big tree for the mere pleasure of winding and there were wood saplings instead of iron railings. The newness of everything, the empty houses where we played hide and seek and the strangeness of it all made us feel that we were living among toys.

Unlike many garden suburbs, though, Bedford Park was not aimed at the skilled working class. There were a large number of middle-class artists, including Lucien Pissarro, brother of the better known Camille. There were also well-off refugees from abroad. The best-known of these was a Russian, who called himself Sergius Stepniak, who was at odds with the Russian government. Whilst on his way to a radical meeting in 1895, however, he was knocked over by a train.

53 (below) View of St Michael's and the TabCard *inn, Bedford Park, 1882.*

54 Woodstock Road, Bedford Park, 1893.

55 Marlborough Crescent, Bedford Park, c.1890.

Victorian Acton was marked by unpleasantness, too. In 1863 there was the shocking murder of PC William Davey at his house in Avenue Road. Long-running nuisances were the piggeries and the brick-making industry. In 1872 there were 18 piggeries in Acton. Many more pigs were kept in houses and killed on unlicensed premises. The smell of boiling fat, offal and blood was certainly unwholesome. The brick-making industry resulted in deposits of filth and refuse as well as the stench of brick fumes, which was thought injurious to health. Bricks were made by mixing clay with burnt fuel extracted from refuse, which ended up in stinking heaps. The Acton Local Board spent much time dealing with these issues, not always successfully. The inspector of nuisances, Isaac Smith, was assaulted by Michael Terry, a pig keeper who had 200 pigs in Osborne Road, when he was about his investigations. Terry was fined four shillings and bound over to keep the peace. The system of dust carts to collect brick rubbish was condemned in the press for failing to call on many premises. In the 1890s the problems became less acute, because building had reduced the amount of land available for brickfields (just one disused one and two which were still operative appear on the 1894 map) and there were fewer piggeries.

But not all of Acton was as awful as this: 'Away in East Acton things have progressed in a more leisurely and peaceful fashion, and a quiet stroll in that neighbourhood will serve, more than anything else, to conjure up before the imagination, Acton's departed beauty' (Perceval Joliffe). On Old Oak Common, in 1870, was founded the People's Garden, run by London's German Club, at which German cultural events were held.

Berrymead Priory had several owners in the 19th century. Edward Bulwer, Lord Lytton, resided here briefly in 1835-6, just after writing *The Last Days of Pompeii*. Shortly afterwards, in 1842, the building was actually used as a Priory, by the Nuns of the Order of the Sacred Heart. Lieutenant Heald, another owner, was bigamously married to Lola Montez, a notorious dancer. In 1882 it appeared that the Priory's days were numbered. It was purchased by the Berkshire Estates Company for £23,000 and the grounds were used to build houses. Fortunately, in 1885 it became home to the Constitutional Club (i.e. Conservative), in whose hands it remained for many decades. 'The average political club is not a thing of beauty and Berrymead Priory stands out among other clubs just as York Chapter House claims to surpass all other chapter houses', reads *The Official Guide to Acton* (c. 1925).

Joliffe passed a mixed judgement on the late Victorian era: 'In conclusion, Acton, particularly during the past quarter of a century, has had its share – perhaps more than its share – of the vast changes incidental to a suburb of a great metropolis. Much that could ill be spared has disappeared, leaving but a memory behind.' Charles Hocking, who arrived in Acton in the 1890s, evocatively recalled scenes of street life of that period:

> Here we would find the costermongers' barrows illuminated by naphtha flares lining the gutter. Stalls of winkles and cockles laid out on little plates with pepper, salt and vinegar at hand; stalls of home made sweets presided over by gypsy women; a German band in shabby hussar uniform playing popular airs; a hurdy-gurdy and monkey; a dancing bear on a chain; the universal street organ … Noise, shouting, pushing, fumes from a naphtha flares … This was the life of work a day Acton, mellowed and refined by memory. An Acton we shall never see again.

Acton changed in the 19th century from a small village with relatively primitive amenities to a rapidly expanding town enjoying basic public services and a whole range of local clubs and shops. Industry became more important, especially the laundries in the south and brickfields in the north. Churches and schools multiplied. Yet, for some, progress must have seemed to be reserved for others.

V

Edwardian Acton, 1901-1914

Trends which had been apparent in the latter part of the 19th century continued at the beginning of the next. Population grew from 37,703 in 1901 to 57,497 in 1911 and there were other important developments in this period. Acton lost even more of its rural character, industry became a major force and the council continued with its efforts to provide public amenities. Acton liked to portray itself almost as an exemplification of the idea of 'Rus in Urbe'. As the *Official Guide to Acton* boasted in *c.*1925,

Within five miles of Marble Arch, Acton has a fitter claim to this title than any other London suburb. On the way to the station in the morning the lark, the thrush, blackbird and robin can be heard, and the flowering trees and shrubs would lead one to believe they were miles in the country, instead of half a mile from the city. Acton is well adapted both for those who like a bracing air and for those who prefer it more relaxing.

This was rather disingenuous. In anticipation of the sharp rise in population, building went on apace. On the West Lodge estate, in West Acton

56 The Smithy, East Acton, c.1905.

on the borders with Ealing, semi-detached
houses were being erected. On the Elms
estate, of about 100 acres, William Daley
and Co. were busy selling detached houses
for £1,250 to £1,350. Semi-detached residences cost £600. Hume and Dennis,
builders, sold semis with four bedrooms
on Buxton Gardens and Lexden Road for
prices as low as £525. The cheapest houses
were in Valetta and Agnes Road, for £325,
though boasting only three bedrooms.
Building was a major industry in Acton in
the 1900s.

Even East Acton began to lose its
hamlet identity as housing began on the
Acton Park estate, which bordered the Uxbridge
Road to the south and East Acton Lane to the
north. The Town and General Estates Company
leased 111 acres and by 1914 had covered half
with houses. There was little housing south of the
Vale, as factories had claimed the land first, but a

57 Old Oak Lane, East Acton, 1900s.

few short terraces were built there at this time.
Housing was also built near to the railway lines to
the north of the parish.

Thomson, in his *Highways and Byways in Middlesex*, was rather critical of Acton:

58 Site of Rosemont Road.

59 *Oldham Terrace,* c.*1900s.*

60 *Old Cottages, Steyne Road,* c.*1904.*

Within recent years these old-time villages have got infected with the virus of civic 'boulimia' and are rapidly devouring the surrounding country. Old houses have been pulled down, old trees felled, old gardens laid waste, and these, in common with the neighbouring fields, have fallen under the influence of the untiring builder.

He added, 'there is little left of antiquity or beauty to appeal to the eye about the neighbourhood now'.

But some rural alcoves remained. These were principally to be found in eastern and northern Acton. East Acton could still be described thus: 'A delightful old-world spot is the country village – for one cannot call it anything else.' It had a village green with a few houses around it and Acton golf course was nearby, temporarily as it turned out, protecting the hamlet from the urban sprawl. The north of Acton was open countryside at this time, which stretched as far as Buckinghamshire and Hertfordshire, 'giving opportunities for walks

and cycle runs in some of the prettiest country near London'. Yet, though there had been little building to the north of the GWR line, construction was proceeding to the railway's immediate south.

According to William King Baker, 'Many of the rustic bits about Acton have already disappeared with the advance of new streets and modern dwellings.' In this period of frantic building, the council bought land in the north and in the south for parks. South Acton Recreation Ground was opened, and its twelve acres of playing fields used for cricket, tennis, football and bowls. Woodlands estate, just off the High Street, was opened as a 'secluded wooded retreat' in 1906. Two years later, with help from the County Council, the twelve acres were purchased for Southfield Road Playing Fields, described by King Baker as 'a valuable lung in this rapidly developing neighbourhood'. In the

61 *Tram running westwards along Uxbridge Road, with council offices in the background, 1900s.*

62 *LUT tram at Shepherd's Bush,* c.*1910.*

63 *Widening Horn Lane for tram use,* c.*1908.*

64 *Tram running westwards along Acton High Street, with railway bridge in the background,* c.*1908*.

65 *The Rectory, Horn Lane, showing overhead tram wires,* c.*1909*.

north of Acton was Acton Playing Fields, of just over 22 acres.

Two developments in transport were seen in Acton in this period, as they were in most other London suburbs: the electric tramway and the motor omnibus. As we have seen, there had been attempts at running a tram service from Shepherd's Bush through Acton and westwards in the 1870s, but with only limited success. In 1901, however, the London United Tramways Company began to operate their line from Shepherd's Bush to Southall, via Acton, Ealing and Hanwell. Three years later it was extended westwards along the Uxbridge Road to Uxbridge and eastwards to Hammersmith. In 1909 the Metropolitan Electric Tramways ran a tram line northwards along Horn Lane to Harlesden, where trams to Finchley and Paddington, amongst other places, could be taken. They were certainly noisy and uncomfortable, but they were faster and more reliable than the horse omnibuses. The latter ceased to operate along the Uxbridge Road by 1908 and they were replaced by motor buses. By 1910

the London General Omnibus Company ran the number 17 from Ealing to Plaistow in Essex through Acton.

'Progress' has a price, and in this instance it had the effect of transforming the High Street. Joliffe wrote of it 'transforming Acton's chief artery into as noisy and busy a thoroughfare as may be found within a five mile radius of London'. The main cause was said to be 'the advent of the electric tram-cars, with their nerve-shattering clang and clatter, and the unseemly turmoil is enhanced by the rush and rattle of the unwieldy and evil-smelling motor omnibus'. The proliferation of transport on the roads also led to a number of accidents. Trams collided in August 1903 on the High Street opposite the Fire Station. Horse-drawn carts, cars and trams crashed into each other on numerous occasions and there was dangerous driving, too. Ralph Dickinson, of Shaa Road, was fined £10 for driving at 35 miles an hour, and the

66 One of the last of the horse buses, 1902.

magistrate said that he wished it had been in his power to levy a more onerous sentence.

Several halts were added to the Great Western railway line in Acton in this decade, as a spur was built northwards from the main line, eventually

67 The Great Bear, no. 111, at Old Oak Common, c.1908.

reaching Northolt. These were at Park Royal (not to be confused with Park Royal on the Metropolitan Line) in 1903, North Acton (1904) and Old Oak Lane (1905). A new shuttle service, run by the District Underground Line, branched off southwards from Acton Town at the already existing South Acton Station in 1905. The Chiswick branch of the North and South Western Junction Railway's line also opened two short-lived halts in Acton, at Rugby Road and at Woodstock Road, to the south-east of the parish, in 1909. Both were permanently closed eight years later.

More unusually, an aerodrome appeared in Acton in these years, one of the first in England. Pioneering flights were made on ground in north-west Acton from at least 1910 and several monoplanes were flown from here. Unfortunately, in 1911, five planes went up in flames, but this did not deter the aviators. In 1913 there was a flying display at Acton. Much of the site's early history is shrouded in darkness, and it is not even marked on the 1914 Ordnance Survey map.

Local government was reorganised and made more professional. Councillor John Jarratt, Chair-

69 The long monoplane at Acton Aerodrome, c.1910.

man of the Council from 1904-6, oversaw most of the changes. He appointed a full-time Town Clerk, this crucial executive post having been held on a part-time basis only, and the first post-holder was William Hobson. A new chief accountant was installed and the accounts and financial department was separated from the Town Clerk's department.

A fierce critic of the council, and its expenditure in particular, was Henry Schultes Young, a lawyer and leading light in the Ratepayers' Protection Party. As a resident of Bedford Park, he attacked anything the council planned which might impinge on the quality of life there, such as a road linking Woodstock Road with other parts of Acton.

Any spending, such as on the new municipal offices, public toilets, fiction for the library and class sizes of less than sixty, came under fire, though not always successfully. No wonder the council said of his activity, 'where all before was peace and concord, he forthwith created strife and conflict'.

One of the more controversial public works was the supply of electricity. As a local authority, Acton had been allowed to supply electricity, to the exclusion of private firms, under a Provision Order of 1890 from the Board of Trade. Nothing had been done about it and the order was to be revoked if such apathy and penny-pinching

68 Thomas Lewis standing by his omnibus, c.1900s.

70 *District Council Offices, 1903.*

71 *Acton Council's electricity department at Wales Farm Road,* c.*1905.*

persisted, when, eventually, an electrical engineer was appointed and a transformer station installed near Wales Farm Road. It began operating in 1905. Very soon, 36 streets were lit by this method. It was found to be an expensive undertaking and, by 1910, there was fierce debate over whether or not the electricity supply should be managed by private enterprise. As might be imagined, Henry Young was a keen advocate of removing the utility from the council's control. It was decided by a narrow margin that it should be consigned to a private company, but this was met by a public outcry. A referendum took place, and the council's motion was just upheld. Acton's electricity would now be supplied by the Metropolitan Electricity Supply Company, who were given a lease for the next 42 years.

72 Henry Monson, architect of many of Acton's public buildings.

73 Procession on behalf of Acton Cottage Hospital, marching along Acton Hill, c.1904.

Other important, though definitely unglamorous, work undertaken in this period was the efficient disposal of rubbish. A dust destructor was eventually housed on Wales Farm Road in order to dispose of the 14,000 tons of rubbish produced annually in the parish. Dust carts were used to pick up rubbish found in the streets, though there were complaints in the press about their lack of efficiency. The vast increase in population put a greater strain on the sewerage services, too. An Act of Parliament was granted in 1905, which allowed the sewage to flow into the LCC's system, and the work making this possible for the southern part of the district was accomplished by 1908.

The expansion of public activity necessitated the proper provision of municipal offices. Land next to the library in the High Street was acquired to this end. The intention was to house all the council's departments on one site. After much wrangling, the foundation stone was laid in 1909

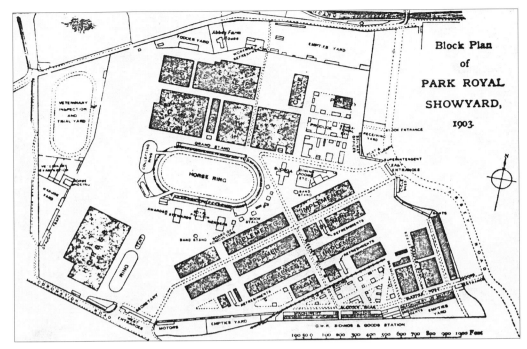

74 *Plan of Park Royal Showyard, 1903.*

and the offices opened in 1910. Acton Council opened a public baths in 1903. These comprised two large baths as well as slipper baths and spray baths. They cost nearly £16,000 (the original estimate had been £100,000 for a rather more grandiose edifice), and were used for concerts in the winter months when the larger bath was equipped with a removable floor.

Although a Cottage Hospital had been established in Acton in the 1890s, there was no public institution for the care of the sick. An isolation hospital at Friar's Place in the north of the parish was established in an existing building, for the care of those afflicted by infectious diseases such as scarlet fever. There were enough beds for 64 patients and it was opened in 1905.

Acton claimed to be a healthy district, with only 13 deaths per thousand of population in 1908. It also claimed to be cheap, with residents paying 7s. 10d. in the pound in rates, somewhat lower than in other districts in Middlesex. Yet infant

mortality, especially among the children of the laundry women, was high, according to a report of 1906. This was due to the poor working conditions and cramped housing people were forced to inhabit.

Apart from the housing, there was another threat to Acton's allegedly rural air. This was not to be fully apparent until after 1918, but it had its roots in pre-war years. King Baker, a reluctant commentator on matters economic, wrote that by 1912, 'south of the Uxbridge Road the motor car industries have established extensive factories', and that there were also 'the printing, dyeing and other works'. The best-known car manufacturer was David Napier and Son. Napier's originated as an engineering company in Soho and later Lambeth. By the 1890s they were experimenting with internal combustion engines. In 1903 the main plant moved to a larger factory in Acton Vale. They built various parts of cars, including several sizes of petrol engines, gear boxes, transmissions and rolling chassis for a variety of cars and other motor vehicles. By 1906 they employed 1,000 men and made about 200 cars per year. There was a lengthy strike at Napier's in the autumn of 1913, beginning in August and lasting until October. Another car manufacturer was Panhard and Levasseur, established on Worple Way by 1909.

A number of other firms relocated to Acton Vale in the first decade of the 20th century. These were often engineering firms who needed land to expand their factories and had also to be near London. E. Bristow, makers of Roundwood cycles, a plate-making factory and a firm of floor makers were all established in the Parade, Acton Vale by 1905. Other large enterprises included Wilkinson Sword Co. Apart from making swords and razors, they also manufactured motor cycles and motor cars. Charles A. Vandervell (CAV) moved his business from Willesden in 1904. His company had pioneered the dynamo-charged battery prin-

ciple by 1908 and created the first public service vehicle lighting system in 1911, which was used to illuminate buses. Other firms included Eastman and Son, which had a dyeworks, and Evershed and Vignoles, makers of electrical equipment.

It was not just around Acton Vale that Acton's industries were concentrated. Park Royal, a manufacturing site to the north of the parish and in the south of Willesden, became the leading industrial zone in west Middlesex, although much of the site had originally been earmarked by the Royal Agricultural Society as a showground; indeed Edward VII had visited the site in 1903. But it was not to be, and by about 1907 the farming interest had lost out and moved elsewhere.

Of Acton's two major industries of the previous century, brick making was in decline and old brickfields became the sites of new factories. The laundries, though, were still in their ascendancy. There were 207 in Acton in 1905. The Pembroke

75 Baldwin's Empire Laundry, The Steyne.

76 Congregational church, 1905.

Laundry in Hazel Road had an average annual turnover of £1,400 between 1907 and 1910, of which £600 was profit and £534 wages. Ten women and five other workers were employed there. One of the largest laundries was the Empire Steam Laundry, whose proprietor from 1905 was Frederick Baldwin. He had a large fleet of vans, first horse-drawn, then motor-powered, and served many districts of west London. Wages, especially in the smaller laundries and where family ties bound the workforce together, were often poor, two or three shillings for a 12-hour day.

Land used for agricultural purposes declined further: in 1901 there were eight cow keepers; in 1914 only two. The 13 piggeries of 1901 had declined to a mere three in 1904. Whereas 137 acres were under arable cultivation in 1890, only 52 of these were still farmed in 1910. Total farmland, including that used for grass, stood at 423 acres in 1910. It had been over 1,000 in 1890.

Little did anyone at the time know, but the seeds of a future supermarket chain were being sown in Acton at this time. Three London grocery assistants, Messrs Waite, Rose and Taylor, together

77 Wesleyan church, The Woodlands, c.1907.

with a little capital and their commercial experience, set up a grocer's shop at 263 Acton High Street in 1904. Four years later, Mr Taylor left and the business expanded to include numbers 265 and 267. The firm became known as Waitrose Ltd. There were downs as well as ups in their first few years, but after the First World War the business was doing well enough to abandon its humble roots and set up stores in well-to-do districts such as Ealing, Kensington and Windsor.

Horn Lane Kinema was the first custom-built picture palace, in 1909. Children stood to watch Saturday afternoon films, while older patrons had afternoon tea whilst they enjoyed the entertainments provided by the silent films. A larger cinema, the Crown at Mill Hill Grove, opened in 1911.

Two new churches were built. Our Lady of Lourdes was the principal Catholic church in Acton, situated on the High Street and opening in 1902. The Anglicans replaced the temporary iron chapel in Hale Gardens with St Martin's church in 1906. It was 'situated in the rapidly developing district on the north side of Ealing road, and [by 1912] has gathered a considerable congregation'. The Bishop of London pointed out at its inauguration that it was important to build churches in areas which were expanding, otherwise if people went without a place of worship for too long they might ignore a new church.

Religious life in Acton was, of course, more than just a matter of bricks and mortar. It manifested itself in many ways. King Baker observed 'of the religious life in Acton ... there has been at least some approach to Christian unity in many directions ... the spirit of Christ has called to unite interest and participation in causes common to all, such as education, temperance, peace and other kinds of social and religious service'. An examination of the parish magazines for St Mary's in 1903 gives an insight into church activities of the time. There were slide lectures, such as one given by the vicar, the Rev. George Sausmarez, entitled 'To Athens and Back'. There were also a number of groups connected to the church, such as the Gleaners' Union, who were involved in supporting overseas missionary work, and there was the Slate Club whose members contributed money as a hedge against sickness and old age. For children there were the Bands of Hope and the Lads' Club, football playing a large part in the latter. 'Pound days' were held regularly when the congregation brought a pound of goods to be sold and the proceeds were sent to a children's home in London. Quarterly meetings of the Mothers' Union were held for mothers 'of all classes'.

A religious survey undertaken by *The Daily News* in 1903 recorded the numbers attending church on one particular Sunday. In Acton there were about 9,000 attenders of services, which was

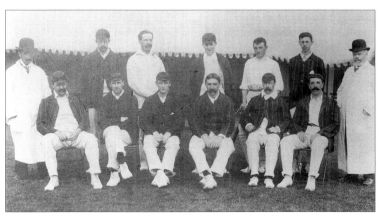

78 Mill Hill Park Cricket Club, 1903.

about one quarter of the whole population. Of these, most were Anglicans, but 427 were Catholics, so the new Catholic church was packed as it could only seat 420. The three quarters of the population who did not attend on that Sunday would have been more infrequent in their attendance.

79 Infants at Southfield Road School, c.1911.

A number of clubs and societies were formed in the 1900s for those with the leisure time to enjoy them. One major annual event was the Horticultural Show. Great numbers participated and categories of entrants included residents, amateurs, ladies and children, showing flowers or plants. Another annual event was the Horse Parade, when horses and carts were decorated and paraded around the town before judges awarded prizes for the best. At least four Boy Scout troops were formed by 1913, mostly affiliated to local churches, and Leopold de Rothschild became their Honorary President. Other clubs were the Photographic Society, the Wesley Guild Lawn Tennis Association and the Acton Town Cricket Club. A branch of the Liberal party was founded.

Several new schools appeared in Acton in these years. According to King Baker, 'The large population in the neighbourhood of Rothschild Road, and the difficulty and delay in procuring sites for new schools necessitated the erection of two iron buildings as temporary schools, in the vicinity.' One of these was Rothschild Road School, initially rather overcrowded although it apparently did well. It was opened in a permanent building in 1912. In the centre of the parish was the new Central School, opened in 1905. The school won athletics prizes and boasted of a cookery centre, science laboratories and a manual training centre for woodwork. Some of its pupils stayed at school after the age of 14. By 1912 it contained accommodation for at least 1,000 pupils.

Two rather prestigious and elite institutions, of a kind Acton had not hitherto known, were the

Haberdashers' Aske's Secondary School for Girls and the Acton County School for Boys. Both provided secondary education, which few other Acton schools did at the time. The Haberdashers' Aske's School (funded by a charitable trust) taught girls from eight to nineteen, preparing them for careers in business or for university. The County School was a similar institution, though for boys aged between ten and nineteen, 'who would receive there the training necessary to fit them for the university, the higher walks of commercial life, and the higher branches of the civil service'. It was controlled and financed by Acton Council and the Middlesex County Council. Both schools were for fee payers, but scholarships were available for suitably bright applicants.

80 Derwentwater School.

81 St Mary's School, Oldham Lane, c.*1900s.*

82 Acton County School, The Woodlands, c.1906.

83 The gymnasium at Haberdashers' Aske's Girls' School, 1900s.

Yet schooling in Acton was far from perfect, nor were its fruits appreciated by all the population. An article in *The Acton Express* of 1903 declared, 'Free education in Acton is apparently of little concern to certain parents in Acton'. Each year, 300 parents were brought up before police courts for the non-attendance of their offspring. The headmaster of the Priory Boys' School frequently commented on the attendance of his pupils, writing comments in the log book such as 'fairly good' and 'rather low'. Absence occurred for a variety of reasons, including wet weather, measles and smallpox and the fact that some of the boys lacked adequate footwear.

Bad behaviour in the town was probably no worse than at any other period, but the press gave it more prominence. Acton had its share of notorious characters as well as the virtuous ones mentioned in King Baker's *History*. In 1903 Charles Hancocks was fined three shillings for appearing drunk and disorderly in the High Street and Elizabeth Stanley, aged 21, was described by the police as 'a well known Acton character' for her unmentionable, though doubtless easily guessable, night-time activities. Boys threw stones at the library's windows and one boy embezzled over five pounds from his master. In Bollo Bridge Road cats were poisoned, and in the High Street bookmakers gathered near the Library. There were fines for men mistreating horses. More seriously, a constable was assaulted. In a town of about 40,000 people, we can easily over-exaggerate these incidents, and it is important to recall that the allegedly halcyon pre-war days were only so in retrospect.

Glimpses of the life of 'ordinary' Actonians can be found in a number of reminiscences. Mabel Woodman recalled leaving school at 14 and going into domestic service at the house of a local schoolmaster. She lived on the premises, rising at six each day to light the fires. She also looked after the children. With board and lodgings, she received five shillings a week. Her escape from this life occurred in 1912 when she married. Amy Rickman left school at about the same age, in 1908. Again, she entered domestic service, staying with her first family for two years, but received a salary of £28 per annum, over twice that of Mabel Woodman.

84 Cock and Crown Yard, c.1905.

Some older buildings were demolished. Derwentwater House in Horn Lane was knocked down in 1909. East Acton's mansion went the same way in 1911. More beneficially, there was a limited degree of slum clearance. The Cock and Crown yard, just off the High Street, was cleared in the same year.

Perhaps one outcome of the great changes in this period are the three histories of Acton that appeared in the years 1910-13: William King Baker's *Acton*, Henry Mitchell's *Records and Recollections of Acton* and Perceval Joliffe's *Acton and its History*. King Baker opened his great book with the following observations: 'Acton Village has become absorbed in the heart of a modern suburb town. Its great houses have nearly all vanished; or, having fulfilled their appointed service, are giving place, one by one, in the presence of the demand for healthy sites and suitable homes.' These histories were written by men who had spent much of their lives in the parish and therefore witnessed at first hand the shift from mid-Victorian village to the built-up suburb of Edward's reign. They concluded that some account of Acton's past should be preserved as the physical remains were fast disappearing.

Some liberal contemporaries believed that a golden age for Acton, and indeed the world, was about to dawn in the second decade of the 20th century. King Baker noted that there had been several meetings of German and English clergymen in Acton in the 1900s, where the virtues of peace and internationalism were proclaimed. One of the German clerics said, 'We needed that better understanding in the great affairs between nations. Those who talk about peace were sometimes regarded as men with their heads in the clouds. But that was not so.' Certainly King Baker believed that the future, especially for his own town, was rosy. On the final page of his book published in 1912, he wrote the following:

> Those who have believed that Acton, hoary with age, has yet a future destined to be still more notable; who believe that greater than the pursuit of any self-interest or sensational prominence, are the lives of unselfish devotion to the public service, and unostentatious loyalty to the truth; who have faith in the broad sweet spirit of tolerance which leads to the kindliness of spirit and deepened appreciation of all that is good and noble in whomsoever found – these may take fresh hope from the substantial progress made in many directions in recent years.

Alas for King Baker, the plans of men in Vienna and Berlin in July 1914 rudely shattered such utopian hopes.

Local trouble and strife manifested itself in a number of ways which were typical of Britain in this period: industrial unrest and militant suffragettes. Efforts to form a laundry workers' union failed and an attempt at the formation of a branch of the National Federation of Women Workers in 1911 was only moderately successful. Likewise, although there was a suffrage march through Acton in 1911, and two years later an Acton suffragette was charged with throwing pepper into Lloyd George's face, there was no independent Acton branch of the suffragettes (the Suffragette Movement was regarded as middle-class). Acton was hardly a middle-class district.

Yet Acton could come together, too. The coronation of George V on 22-4 June 1911 was a major event. The council formed a committee to organise municipal rejoicing, and there were festivities in Acton Park on Coronation Day which were so successful that about 40,000 people (almost the entire population) attended them. A new bandstand was erected there and the King

85 *Opening of new bandstand in Acton Park to celebrate the coronation of George V, 1911.*

86 Unlocking of new gate at Acton Park by Mrs Boissiounade as part of the coronation celebrations, 1911.

George V Ornamental Garden was opened just off the High Street. In the Central Hall, 373 elderly people were given a special tea. A huge bonfire was lit at North Acton, one of a long chain of beacons lit across the country. As King Baker remarked, 'It was a magnificent spectacle – a fitting finish to the great day's rejoicings.'

By the eve of the Great War, Acton had developed into a bustling industrial town. There were strenuous efforts at making both secular and religious provision for the people. On the other hand, there were also disputes, petty crime, poverty and traffic accidents. It was an era of great change, often for the better, though not always so.

VI

The First World War

The First World War posed a serious challenge to a country which had known general peace for many decades and Acton faced many demands in the four years of total conflict. Apart from the need for manpower for the armed forces, there were fears on the Home Front of bombing and food shortages.

At first enlistment was voluntary and there seem to have been two main forms of appeal to the men of Acton. A number of recruitment parades took place in the town in 1914-15. One, in December 1914, involved a march with local brass bands from the Council Offices along the Uxbridge Road and ending at East Acton village. Speeches were made by the chairman of the council and other civil dignitaries. The second form was advertisements in *The Acton Gazette*. One such in February 1915 asked, 'Do you feel happy? Do you feel happy as you walk along the streets and see other men wearing the King's uniform? If not, why don't you enlist today and do your share?' Recruits, unmarried men between 18 and 30 and in good physical condition, presented themselves at the recruiting office in the Council Offices. Those who had been employed by the council would continue to receive their civilian wage minus whatever the Army gave them. Recruitment seemed to work well, at least at first. Between 7 and 31 August 375 local men joined up. In the first three days of September another 120 did so. This flow of recruits was maintained throughout 1915.

Conscription was introduced in January 1916 amidst much political controversy. Those who objected to military service had their cases heard before the Acton Military Tribunal, made up mostly of councillors. King Baker, a noted pacifist and councillor, defended his three sons, all of whom refused to fight, although eventually one was obliged to serve in the Medical Corps. Shopkeepers and small businessmen were usually granted a few months to put their commercial affairs in order before joining up. Conscientious objectors, who refused to fight for religious reasons, were not popular. Rifleman Smith thought their arguments were 'piffling rot', and 'Disgusted' of Acton said that objectors only lived in peace because of the Army and therefore should enlist to help defend the weak.

A total of 718 of those who fought were killed. Of these, three were awarded the Military Cross, seven the Military Medal and one the Distinguished Service Medal. Newspaper columns about the men who became casualties became very frequent from the middle of 1915 onwards. One of the first to die was Private Robins, aged 28, of the 2nd Dragoon Guards, killed in Flanders on 13 May 1915. As a reservist he had been called up in August 1914. In his last letter home he wrote:

> Now the good weather is here at last, I hope this will be over by the end of the summer. If not, well, another winter! ... I live in hopes of meeting again as I have an idea in my head I shall get back

87 *Tea party in Acton in aid of injured soldiers, 1916.*

safe and sound. The three boys from Acton Green are still well, and have been out here since it began.

Lieutenant Allastair McReady-Diarmid of the Middlesex Regiment was the town's one recipient of the Victoria Cross. On 1 December 1917 he led his company through a barrage of enemy fire and drove the Germans back 300 yards, capturing 27 of them in the process. On the following day a similar exploit was achieved. McReady-Diarmid fought at the head of his company, throwing bombs towards the enemy in order that his men might advance more safely. Unfortunately he was killed, and it was said, 'His heroism is the talk of the Brigade'. Before the war he had lived at Goldsmiths' Avenue, and he enlisted in March 1915.

Acton's soldiers seem to have been supported by their friends and families on the Home Front.

Money was raised for the war effort by the Acton War Savings Committee, which encouraged people to lend money to the government by purchasing war bonds and national savings certificates. In 1917 Acton raised £96,388 by this method. There were lectures in the town to help promote such saving, and a Tank Day on 12 March 1918 when a tank drove around Acton with a procession of Boy Scouts, cadets and members of the St John Ambulance. Herbert Nield, MP for the Middlesex Division, made a speech about the need for a just peace. The event was a great success and a total of £134,129 was subscribed on that day alone.

An Acton Relief Fund was formed and appealed for subscriptions, and with this money those suffering financial hardship due to the war were helped. Boy Scouts helped guard reservoirs and collected waste paper. Tradesmen and older men enrolled as Special Constables to supplement the regular police as many of the latter rushed to the colours. Food parcels and other gifts were sent to the troops at the Front. Girls from St Mary's School sewed items for the soldiers. A number of Belgian refugees, fleeing the German invasion of their country, were given shelter in Acton, and local people gave money to assist them. At the Central School, a 'Pound Day' was held in November 1914 to raise funds for the refugees, who were housed at Acacia Road and Perryn Road: 'It was a great success and a very large amount of food stuffs was divided between the two homes as a result.'

Local patriotism had an ugly side too, as all things German were, understandably, demonised. Shortly after the war broke out, the pub, the *Crown Prince of Prussia*, changed its name to the *Crown Prince of Russia*. Rather more seriously, in May 1915, just after the *Lusitania* was sunk (in which vessel there were two Acton men – one drowned), there had been outbursts of anti-German rioting in Liverpool and London. Six shops in Acton owned or run by Germans were attacked. Crowds of women, men and boys surrounded the buildings and threw missiles and abuse. The local police and special constables were not entirely unsympathetic towards the crowds, but eventually arrested some of them. The rioters were dealt with leniently.

Acton Aerodrome is thought to have seen active service during the war. Certainly aircraft are reported to have been flying from here in that period. Volunteer troops guarded the premises. More is known of the site in 1917-18 when it was used by the Ruffy-Baumann Flying School, an establishment headed by an Italian and two Swiss brothers, plus a team of English, French and Italian instructors. They trained men to fly the biplanes which operated from here and received money from the government to do so. Pupils included Captain Albert Hall, VC, and Lord Balfour. In the summer of 1918 the flying school was disbanded

88 William Poore, special constable, 1914.

89 James Pearson, pupil at Ruffy Baumann Flying School, c.1917.

and the site taken over by the Alliance Factory in
order to manufacture aircraft, but the plant may
not have been built until the following year and it
is probable that not many fighting aircraft for the
First World War were made here.

90 *Military aircraft at Acton Aerodrome.*

91 *French S.P.A.D. biplane at Acton.*

One Acton firm which made large
numbers of military vehicles was
Napier's. Red Cross ambulances boasted
Napier chassis. Delivery vans made by
Napier's were able to use gas bags in
order to save fuel. Three and a half ton
trucks were supplied to the British and
the Russian armies. Aero engines were
made here from 1914 under government
contract. In November 1917 the firm's
efforts were rewarded by a royal visit by
George V. Other companies turned

92 Two women workers at Acton Aerodrome.

metaphorical plough shares into swords. Wilkinson's increased their output of swords for officers and made bayonets (about two and a quarter million in all, mainly the work of female employees) for the other ranks. Evershed and Vignoles made steering and target equipment for the Royal Navy. The Ogston Motor Company made travelling kitchens for the Forces at the rate of six a week in 1915. Many munitions factories moved to the empty land at Park Royal where there was a large horse compound for the Royal Army Service Corps. Some factories moved there in the summer of 1918 but soon shut down as the end of the war was in sight. Dorothy Crowther was the war's only known female casualty, a 16-year-old who was working in a munitions factory when she was killed in a tragic accident in 1918.

There were mortal dangers to the civilian population, too, which was hitherto almost unknown. In 1915 the Germans began to use zeppelins and,

93 Business as usual: Acton High Street, c.1917.

94 *Men at work on Ealing to Shepherd's Bush line, 1915.*

95 *'Cheesewring', no. 1311, at Old Oak Common, c.1917.*

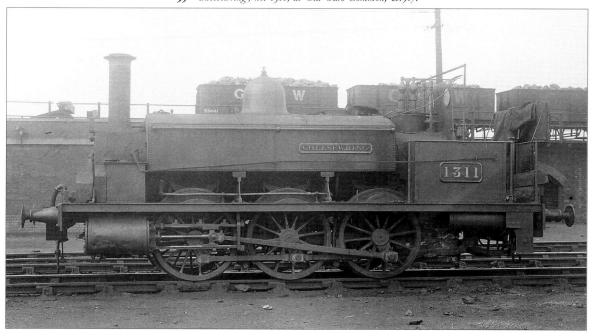

96 CAV Football Club, c.1917.

later, aircraft to bomb Britain. According to the Acton Central School log book, on 3 October 1917, 'Timetable suspended from 1.15 to 2.00 … during air raid take cover period. There was no sign of gunfire on the ground'. At St Mary's School, attendance on 5 October 1917 was poor because of the air raids. Some children were sent out of Acton for a time.

Few air-raid shelters were constructed. Wilkinson Sword made one for their employees and a councillor made one in his garden. The Napier works had organised their own branch of the St John Ambulance Brigade by 1917 and were able to use one of their own one-ton vans. There was a works fire brigade, too. On the whole, the plan was that people should be directed to their own homes or allowed to shelter in public buildings during the raids. Hundreds in Britain died during them, and one man in Acton died of his wounds caused by the bombing. There were reports of

two people dying from indirect effects. Harry Thrould, aged 61, had a heart attack owing to one of the raids, and a middle-aged woman drowned herself because of anxiety over the bombing.

There were other hardships on the Home Front. Partly because of the German submarine campaign against the Merchant Navy, food shortages became a problem in the later years of the war. The Acton Poultry Association managed to rear 1,000 fowls, and Acton's agricultural demise was briefly halted. The council opened two National Kitchens in 1917 to provide subsidised lunchtime meals. In March 1918, 1,500 of these were provided. Efforts were made thereafter to double output. Sugar rationing was introduced in January 1918, with sugar only legally available at four shops in Acton. Vacant land in East Acton Lane and Old Oak Road was used for allotments. In Acton Park, potatoes were grown instead of flowers. The war drove prices up, with the result that there was

97 *Victory Parade along Acton High Street, 1919.*

pressure for increased wages among council staff. War bonuses of up to an additional 20 shillings a week were given to employees by 1918.

Peace came at last on 11 November 1918, when Germany signed the armistice. At twenty past nine in the morning, the coming of peace was being whispered at the Post Office and the rumour spread to the Council Offices and then more generally throughout the town. People on buses congratulated each other and waved and cheered from the tops of trams. Shop assistants and traders gathered outside their shops. Flags were hung out and bugles blown. Rockets were fired at half past ten.

The Acton Gazette was critical of these spontaneous rejoicings, probably in part on account of its campaign to see Acton incorporated as a borough. 'A good many, of course, ran off to London, but Acton, as a whole, had to rejoice locally, and there was a certain carelessness about a good deal of rejoicing, nobody quite knowing

98 Unveiling of War Memorial at the Cemetery, 1927.

99 War Memorial book of fallen Actonians.

what to do.' If it was careless, it was also heartfelt. Crowds of female munitions workers and others downed tools and took to the streets, singing and dancing. Works closed at lunchtime. Even the drizzle did not dampen spirits as cadets of the County School played drums and bugles in a tangled procession with discharged soldiers. There were still crowds in the streets in the evening, despite the rain; whizz-bangs were fired and church bells rung. The special constables were on duty but there was no disorder.

The official peace celebrations occurred on 19 July 1919. According to *The Acton Gazette*, 'the town was well beflagged, with here and there appropriate mottoes'. There was a mass display in Acton Park by the local boy scouts, who were inspected by Sir Harry Brittain, Acton's first MP. Many, though, went up to London for celebrations on a rather larger scale. The Cottage Hospital was expanded by public subscriptions as a practical and public war memorial. There was also a memorial unveiled in Acton Cemetery on 25 June 1927.

VII

Suburban Acton

Whether Acton was 'a very desirable centre in which to take up one's abode' in the inter-war years, as the borough guide of 1925 claimed, is debatable. According to Martin Briggs, writing in 1934, Acton did not appear very prepossessing. He referred to 'The crowded borough of Acton … this apparently mediocre and suburban township'; yet he also noted it had 'a keen civic sense'.

One of the most important developments in Acton in the 1920s was incorporation in October 1921. Several urban district councils in Middlesex had become municipal boroughs since Ealing took the lead in 1901. Acton's new council had a mayor, eight aldermen and 24 councillors, the borough now being divided into four wards for electoral purposes. Since the Acton Chamber of Commerce was prominent in the movement to make Acton a borough, perhaps it was unsurprising that the first mayor was Alderman Frederick Baldwin (1855-1924), a leading local businessman. Baldwin's was a success story, from office boy in the City to the owner of the Empire Steam Laundry and Charter Mayor of Acton. Another early mayor was Miss Susan Smee, who was the first woman to hold that post of honour, in 1924.

The borough guide commented on the incorporation:

> This was, of course, a natural recognition of Acton's large population and the commercial and industrial importance of the town. From this great milestone in the local history the town may be expected to make rapid all round progress, for the possession of full civic rights is not merely a legal convenience for practical purpose but a great stimulus to local pride and public spirit.

It certainly seemed to give Acton a greater degree of self pride and a focus for local loyalties.

Another important development which recognised Acton's increased importance was its

100 *Charter Procession along Acton High Street, 1921.*

becoming a Parliamentary Borough in 1918 (previously it had been part of the Ealing division of Middlesex). Apart from 1929-31, Acton's MPs in this period were always Conservative. Sir Harry Brittain served for the longest period, from 1918-29. He was very eager to foster links between Acton and its namesake in Canada. In 1924 he met Judge Moore from Acton, Canada, which led to the exchange of plaques of each other's coats of arms. Brittain remarked, 'I am a great believer in these little links of sentiment between those of the Motherland and their namesake towns overseas.' Politically, this period saw a quiet revolution in the make up of the council. The Ratepayers' Association, a strong force in pre-war politics, became defunct in 1921 and the Labour Party emerged as a potent force to battle the local Conservatives, whilst the Liberals were squeezed out – there was only one Acton Liberal Club left by 1930.

101 Councillor and Mrs Mence, mayor and mayoress of Acton, 1929.

102 The Rev. John Crowlesmith, mayor's chaplain, 1933-4

A snapshot of Acton's population can be garnered from the 1921 census. There were 28,317 men and 32,982 women, the difference in part being due to war casualties. In some matters, Acton's statistics were similar to those for the rest of the county of Middlesex. There were 5.73 people to each house and 1.3 families in each dwelling place. Men were on average aged 29.5 and women 31.4. Yet in one way Acton was very atypical: there were 26.6 people per acre, compared with a county average of 8.4. This meant that Acton had one of the highest population densities in the county. Although most of the population were from the British Isles, several hundred had been born in Europe (mostly France or Germany, though there were also nine Poles), 20 were from Asia and there was one African (probably expatriate whites).

Housing was a major concern in this growing factory town. In 1931 there were 70,510 people, the highest that Acton's population ever numbered. Density per acre was 30.2 persons. The state of housing in the Steyne had long been condemned for being unsatisfactory, but little action had been taken. In 1927 it was reported that one family had lived in a single room in one of these houses for six years. In 1935 much of it was demolished and replaced in 1938 by a four-storey block of flats called Steyne House.

One thousand working-class houses were built on a number of sites in the 1920s, by the council as well as by private builders. Flats were also built, but by the end of the 1930s there was still some degree of overcrowding. Some of the housing was good, some less so. Briggs refers to 'the drab streets of [the] southern quarter', but also to 'the charming

Garden Village of the Great Western Railway … The excellence of these various schemes makes one wish that more artistic sense, and indeed more commonsense, had been exercised in developing other parts of the borough.' Little new housing could be built by the 1930s, though, because there was little farm land left on which to build. Acton's numbers ceased to grow. Acton Council did its limited bit in 'making homes fit for heroes', with the erection of 328 houses and 187 flats 'for the artisan classes' between 1919 and 1939.

The cheapest houses, such as those in the housing estate called the East Acton Village, cost about £600, and this was after a government

103 Railway Cottages, Stephenson Street, 1920s.

104 Bull's Head Inn, *East Acton Lane, 1920.*

subsidy had been awarded in 1926. Bungalows in Lowfield Road cost £600 in 1923, though on the more expensive scale were houses in Noel Road at £800 or Cecil Road at £1,000. A large house on Acacia Road with a garage and a garden cost £1,650 in 1928. Most two-bedroom homes were £825. Council house schemes were not always popular. When the council decided to build houses on Canada Road in 1933, some ratepayers protested. The total cost to buy land and build 54 houses was £26,000 and the ratepayers would have to contribute nearly a fifth of this amount. Despite protests, the houses were erected in 1935. Other major builders in north and east Acton in this era were the Victory Construction Company, who built 70 bungalows, and the Great Western Village Society, who built houses for their employees in 1923-4.

East Acton, which had been a hamlet since the Middle Ages, became part of the dense suburban mass that was Acton after the golf course was built on following its purchase by the council in 1919. Some land, though, was saved for use as parkland. By 1925, there were 84 acres of parks in Acton. Southfields Road Recreation Ground was opened in 1923 and Wesley Playing Fields in 1931. There was about 100 acres of open space in Acton by 1939.

The 1921 census gives an indication of how Acton adults were employed. Of the 19,000 working men, the largest number in one form of occupation were the 2,768 metal workers, mostly in the car manufacturing plants in the town. A close second were the 2,729 who worked in transport-related industries, unsurprising given the tram depot and the number of train and bus routes through the town. Outside the borough were the Chiswick Bus Works and the Acton Railway Works, which employed numbers of men from Acton. Other common categories included office workers, many of whom probably worked in London as well as locally. Fewer women were employed, only

105 Additional building at the Cottage Hospital, 1920s.

106 Foundation stone for nurses' home at the Cottage Hospital, c.1930.

9,737 out of a total of 26,554 aged over twelve. Unsurprisingly, given Acton's reputation as Soapsud Island, 1,827 worked in the laundry trade. Many working women were in domestic service, 1,754 in all. Women also worked in offices as clerks and typists, to the number of 1,437.

The Cottage Hospital increased the number of its beds from 35 in 1920 to 72 in 1935. The extension to the hospital, built in 1922-3 and opened by Neville Chamberlain, was a memorial to the men killed in the war. The Isolation Hospital almost trebled its accommodation. More serious problems were dealt with at Isleworth or at the Central Middlesex Hospital in Park Royal. A new and improved Fire Station was opened on Gunnersbury Lane in 1938 and, perhaps with the possibility of the coming war in mind, underground shelters were built.

Leisure facilities, many of them provided by local firms, soared in number in this era. There were 17 athletics, 15 tennis and four cricket clubs. Though there had been two cinemas in Acton before 1914, by 1939 there were briefly six (one closed in 1939, another in 1940). One of these, The Globe, opened in 1921, was in the High Street and was said to be the largest in the country, seating 3,000 people. It was built mostly by local men, the architect and main contractors all being Actonians. Cinemas played an important role in the lives of many in this era and were often recalled with affection. Reg Dunckling recalled that as a lad in the 1930s a visit to the cinema cost tuppence, but some sneaked in via side entrances or the toilets to see a film for free.

Acton's football team was founded in 1936 as a boys' club. It was very much an amateur undertaking, playing friendly games and using hats and coats as goal posts, but it quickly moved to greater things. In 1937 it entered the Thames Valley Minor

107 Mill Hill Park cricket team, 1929.

League and Association, and just before the war it won the Thames Valley Minor League Championship and Founder's Cup. However, hopes of glory were dashed with the outbreak of war and the closure of the club. In South Acton, many supported Brentford or their rival, Queen's Park Rangers.

Acton's first public telephone box appeared in about 1925 on the south-west corner of the Mount. Those few private individuals who had a telephone at home were wired up to either the Chiswick or Shepherd's Bush exchange. It was not until 1931 that Acton had its own exchange, which was in Lexden Road and was called The Acorn – the name 'Acton' deriving from 'oak-town'. Most, though not all, businesses in Acton possessed telephones by this time.

Perhaps the most prominent building in Acton was the Ministry of Pensions office near Bromyard Avenue, which was said to be the largest building in the country under a single roof. Work was begun on it in 1914, but because of the interruptions

caused by war, it was not completed until 1922. Another significant structure was the new Town Hall, completed in 1939, which was really only an extension of the Municipal Offices on the High Street, and cost £96,000, far more than the original building had done.

Although Gunnersbury Park is within Ealing's boundaries, this has not prevented some writers from appropriating it to Brentford, Chiswick or Acton. This early 19th-century mansion and its large grounds had belonged to the Rothschilds, who owned land in Acton and proved worthy benefactors therein. In 1925 Acton and Ealing councils acquired it for use as a local museum and its grounds of 186 acres as a park. It was opened to the public by the Minister of Health, Neville Chamberlain, on 21 May 1926. A year later, Brentford and Chiswick councils took a share in administering the Park.

There was considerable relocation of industry towards Acton between the wars. Building

108 Outings of staff at Thistle Laundry, 1920s.

109 *Acton Town Hall, completed 1939.*

regulations were less strict in Middlesex than in London, and since Acton Vale was just outside the boundaries of London County Council it was an ideal location. Furthermore, there was the excellence of its transport links (especially the railways), and its proximity to London was useful as regards both markets and labour supply.

It would be impossible to list every firm which existed in Acton, but the variety of industry was immense. Landis and Gyr occupied premises in Victoria Road from 1927, making meters for the measurement of energy consumption in the home and for industry. By 1932 there were 28 factories on Victoria Road. Thomas Wall had a large factory built near Friar's Place in 1919, which was soon known as the Friary. It manufactured both sausage meat and ice cream, both of which were world famous. In 1922 the first 'Stop me and buy One' tricycles operated from the factory. Edward

Saunders and Son Ltd had been making wrapping materials since 1832, and established themselves in Acton in 1929, the year of the Wall Street crash. Another manufacturer of paper products was Harold Wesley Ltd, with a factory on Acton Lane from 1924. There were also firms which made chromium plating, zinc alloy for rustproofing, shoe soles and heels, and wire connectors, to name a handful. In the early 1920s it was noted, 'Acton has that variety of industry which makes for commercial stability and avoids those sharp contrasts of depression and prosperity which come to towns relying upon one or two staple industries'.

Park Royal was developed in this era, in the area straddling north Acton and Willesden. The major manufacturer here was the Guinness brewery, which bought up large tracts of land to ensure the firm could select which industries rented land for factory space near the brewery. Industrial estates full of modern factories powered by electricity sprang up. There were no smoking chimneys and smog here, as there was in much of London. Development on the Park Royal estate was aided by the building of the nearby Western Avenue.

There were also changes in the laundry industry. In 1920 there were 160 laundries, but by 1922 this had fallen to 130, about 120 by 1933, and 90 by 1939. Yet 1,800 families had one member or more involved in the trade in 1921. Furthermore, Acton had a section all to itself in the trade journal devoted to the industry. By this time motor vans were taking clothes to and from the laundries.

Trade was given a boost in 1928 when a covered market was opened in Crown Street. It was alleged to be the largest and cheapest such market in western London. Mr Whittleton, a bank clerk, recalled, 'Crown Street with its street market was always an attraction and in the evenings, with naptha lights spluttering over the stalls, there was an atmosphere not found today.' Messrs Hawkins and Orford, who later developed a large grocery business, started here, offering free tea and milk to draw in customers. Another character was 'Scotty', who sold linen and towels, gathering a crowd by his banter. There were few department stores in Acton in this period. Individual service, as opposed to catering for a mass market, was deemed more important. The Maypole Dairy cut its butter to the size asked for; butchers cut bacon according to personal wishes. Bakers stores displayed their unpackaged wares through glass containers; Mr Bowbeer, a butcher, claimed he sent his sausages to Paris by air.

The construction of the Western Avenue was planned by the Middlesex County Council with help from the Ministry of Transport. It was decided

110 Park Royal Station railway bridge, c.1925.

that a road was needed from London to the west which would bypass the existing Uxbridge Road. It was to begin at Old Oak common and end near Denham in Buckinghamshire. Discussion first took place in 1913, but war intervened and it was not until 1921 that construction began, using otherwise unemployed men. By 1929 the road had reached Hanger Lane; it extended as far as Greenford in 1934 and eventually reached east Buckinghamshire in 1943. Acton now had two major thoroughfares.

Passenger transport was also improved. The Central Underground Line was extended as far west as Ealing Broadway in 1923, with two stations being built in Acton (West Acton and North Acton). East Acton station, built in 1920, is actually in Hammersmith. The Piccadilly line also went through Acton in 1932, and could be accessed via Acton Town Station.

There was little bus transport in Acton before 1914. In the early 1920s there were a large number of independent ('pirate') operators, one-man buses, some driven by ex-soldiers who had used their army pay to buy a bus. The result was colourful but chaotic, as the buses plied the profitable route along the Uxbridge Road. The London General

Omnibus Company was their main rival. It vastly increased the number of routes its buses served. There had been only one bus route before 1914, but in 1928 there were six on weekdays and five on Sundays. They travelled to most parts of London – as far as Liverpool Street, Lower Sydenham, Southall, Harlesden and Euston. The company began to take over some of the 'pirates' throughout the 1920s, but in 1933 itself succumbed to London Transport, which gained control of all the capital's transport services. Despite the innovation of a tramway from Acton to Putney in 1928, trams were replaced in Acton by trolley buses in 1936.

A number of new churches and schools opened in this period. These included, for the Anglicans, St Gabriel's in north Acton and St Saviour's in 1927. There was a new Baptist chapel at East Acton Lane in 1931 and one for the Methodists at the Fairway, Old Oak, in 1926. In the same year, the Salvation Army opened its Citadel in Crown Street. Acton Technical College was founded in 1928 and played its part in fostering local industries by training young men, totalling 3,912 (many of whom were part-time), in 1938-9. Berrymead Middle School, South Acton and John Perryn First and Middle School in East Acton opened in 1931, West Acton First in 1937. Montessori methods were used in the infant classes, educational apparatus being used in a more structured way than in traditional methods of teaching. The Italian founder of the system, Dr Montessori, visited Acton schools in 1929 and was pleased to see how her ideas were being implemented.

III Infants at West Acton School, 1937.

112 Masters and boys of *Acton County School,* c.*1930s.*

113 Schools football final, *Acton Priory v. Acton Central, 1931. Priory won, 2 goals to nil.*

Everyday life in Acton County School is captured in the diaries of Henry St John, the only son of a Chiswick shopkeeper, who attended as a scholarship boy from 1922-7. Being poor at games and finding homework difficult made for an unhappy school life. Yet he was able to matriculate in 1927 and pursue a career in the civil service. There are a number of reminiscences of Acton residents which shed light on working life at this time. Helen Leader, who worked at Acton bakeries in the 1930s as a junior clerk, recalled that the

dressing up in costumes worn during the reigns of the first four King Georges (1714-1830). There were children's festivities and a high tea for the old people. The whole event cost £1,821. During school holidays on 6-7 May, the borough's children were presented by the mayor with jubilee medals. The children of the Priory boys' school were treated, on 8 May, to a trip to the Crown Cinema, a variety entertainment at the school hall, then a tea with party food. Unsurprisingly, 290 out of 292 attended. Sadly, a year later the old King died,

114 Nevill's Bakery, vehicle fleet, 1930s.

deliverymen had to collect their loads at 5 a.m. and work on Saturdays and public holidays. The business began on the Vale and grew; there were eventually 12 shops serving Acton and the surrounding districts. Mabel Woodman recalled that her husband, who worked in the laundry trade, drove the van and did some washing. Laundry was delivered in baskets. On busy days, Mabel would help from 9 a.m. to 8 p.m.

One great occasion in this period was the Silver Jubilee of George V in 1935. The main event was the Pageant of the Five Georges held on 6 May in Gunnersbury Park, which involved participants

and there was widespread grief and messages of sympathy from various local organisations.

Perhaps the most alarming event for the town was the outbreak of the General Strike in May 1926, following a breakdown in relations between the different sides of the coal industry, which resulted in the TUC calling on all its members to lay down their tools. Since Acton was very much a hub of the transport industry it was particularly affected. Men employed on the railways, trams and buses ceased to work. For Henry St John this meant that he walked to school rather than take the District railway line, and either walked back or took

a 'most perilous return journey on Gibson's bike'.
Bus stations and District railway stations in Acton
were closed; the latter reopened on the 11th but
the service was initially unreliable. Pirate
buses ran along the Uxbridge Road and
the council decided to stop pending
prosecutions against them. Volunteers
ran other buses, trains and trams until
13 May, which was seen as a potentially
dangerous enterprise. Two trams crashed
into one another on the 13th, one driven
by volunteers. St John observed, 'Buses
now have barbed wire round bonnets to
prevent destruction of the engine.'

Most people seem to have made
unusual efforts to reach their workplaces;
two teachers were absent from the Priory
School on 4 May owing to 'difficulties
of transport', but they turned up two

115 Factory floor of Napier's, c.1920.

116 Workers at Neal's, Park Royal, 1936.

days later. Drivers gave lifts to those
walking along the Uxbridge Road to
London. Mr Clarke, headmaster of Acton
County School, said, 'he despised any boy
who, within walking distance, could not
come to school because of the strike'.

On 4 May, men from the Acton and
Ealing branches of the National Union
of Railwaymen and other strikers gathered
on Ealing Common. They were addressed
by a Labour councillor and a Welsh miner,
then marched with banners flying and
band playing, through Ealing. There was
another mass meeting of 4,000 men five
days later. There was little recorded
violence, apart from verbal abuse aimed
at those driving buses and trams. A
motorist offering a man a lift was
answered, 'I'll give you a lift under the
jaw!' A passenger alighting from a tram
on Acton High Street was assaulted by a
navvy. There was a sense of emergency
in the air. St John recorded on 3 May,
'Saw troops with tin helmets and rifles
taken to London'. Two days later he wrote,
'Revolution seems imminent. 3000 troops
with fixed bayonets and machine guns
reported to be at London General
Omnibus Company Works, Gunnersbury'. This turned out to be alarmist,
although it was a view shared by others.

The council was concerned about the
supply and distribution of essential goods, basically
food and coal. A special committee was formed,
headed by the mayor, to oversee such matters. It
had its insurance policies on public buildings
extended to include riot damage. The Food
Emergency Office it set up did not last long, closing
on 20 May, a week after the strike was called off.
South Acton railwaymen returned to work on
14 May, two days after the strike officially ended.

117 Neal's works and railway sidings, 1930s.

118 Neal's stand at a building exhibition, 1936.

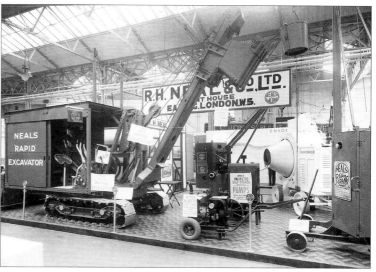

St John wrote, 'One of our communists [said] to
me, "Comrade, I hope you're pleased with this
result of capitalism".'

There were three other major causes of
concern, some of which had their origins overseas.
The first was the growth of local fascism. In 1925
a company of British Fascists was formed in Acton.
Although they were anti-communist, they did not
parade the town in black shirts and many of their

activities seem rather innocent, such as Friday night dances and whist drives. Rather more serious were the activities of the Acton branch of Mosley's British Union of Fascists, founded in 1932, including skirmishes with socialists at open-air meetings and the adoption of a candidate to fight the parliamentary election scheduled for 1940

(which never occurred). Yet, for all its noise, fascism was not a significant force in Acton.

Unemployment was a scourge which affected most of Britain in the inter-war years, even in towns in the south of England where new industries were booming. A slump followed the initial post-war boom. In 1921, after the official procession to mark

119 Shop window display at the corner of Church Road and High Street, c.1930.

120 Shops on Acton Hill, 1920s.

121 Acton Market, Crown Street, 1928.

122 *General strikers meet on Ealing Common, 1926.*

123 *Bus driven by volunteer during General Strike, 1926.*

the incorporation of Acton, there was an unofficial procession of the local unemployed. In 1923 there were 800 unemployed in Acton. Ten years later there was little change, with local men taking part in hunger marches to Isleworth. In 1933 a branch of the National Unemployed Union was formed. Mr Whittleton recalled the Labour Exchange in the High Street: 'in times of unemployment in the '30s it was depressing to see the queues there.'

There were local schemes to alleviate the worst effects. The council gave coal tickets and provided

124 Acton's unemployed queue outside the employment exchange on the High Street, 1931.

free baths to the families of the unemployed. Public works, such as employing men to widen the roads, was a useful short-term solution. Premises were opened to men who would otherwise have nowhere to go. Voluntary bodies such as the Rotary Club and the Social Council pressurised the council to do more as regards direct relief. Finally, Edward VIII, thought to be sympathetic to the lot of the poor, visited the training centre for the unemployed at Gorst Road in June 1936.

In the mid- and late 1930s there were a number of crises across Europe which threatened the peace of the continent, and many thought bombardment from the air was the greatest danger to the civil population. In 1936-7 air-raid precautions were discussed by Acton Council and in the local press. In May 1937 there was talk of appointment of an ARP officer to co-ordinate civil defence, but it was not until January 1938 that one Major Stevens

took up his post. Two months later there were 300 volunteer ARP wardens, and, by March 1939, 500 men had received training. A month earlier gas masks had been distributed, but some were found to be faulty. Men also trained to form anti-aircraft battery crews and in April 1939 they held their annual dinner. Women were involved, forming an ATS unit in January 1939. Although one shelter was built in Lowfield Road in 1938, no others were completed until 1940.

In some ways, the 1920s were a high point for Acton. It was now both a parliamentary borough and a municipal borough. For its residents there were some material improvements, though the depression affected many and fear of a coming war hung like a cloud in the late 1930s. There was overcrowding, too, though it is probable that the relentless rise in numbers had reached its limit and was beginning to fall off.

VIII

The Second World War

Unlike many industrial parts of London and its environs, Acton was not too badly bombed during the Blitz and subsequent air attacks on England. Yet the civilian population was just as engaged in the struggle as the threat of invasion and the peril of aerial bombing loomed higher than in the previous war. Almost as soon as Germany invaded Poland in September 1939, pre-war plans for the evacuation of schoolchildren were put in motion. Acton Central station was thronged with mothers and children from all of Acton's schools about to depart for Dorset and Devon. One schoolgirl from the Central School recorded that the boys were sent to Dartmouth and the girls to Kingsbridge. Teachers had to commute between the two places to conduct their lessons. West Acton Infants' School went to Holberton in Devon.

Hundreds flocked to recruiting stations and young couples went to registry offices. Sandbags were filled by dozens of volunteers and placed around public buildings such as the hospitals. ARP posts were constructed and trenches dug on Acton Green. *The Acton Gazette* tried to promote a sense of calm, by stating 'this country has never been better protected', which might have been true but it overlooked the fact that never before was it to be subject to such a massive aerial bombardment.

It is not certain how many Acton men died on active service. *The Acton Gazette* carried reports of 116, and even if this is not complete it is nevertheless far fewer than had died in the First World War. They had seen service in the many campaigns

of the war: in France in 1940 and 1944, the Far East, the Western Desert and in Italy. Although none won the VC, there were numerous acts of bravery which included Private Smith winning the Military Medal, in Palestine in 1940, Corporal Charles George killing 14 Japanese in Burma in 1944 and Corporal Fred Barrett being wounded after capturing five Germans in the same year. There were 558 registered conscientious objectors in Acton.

Henry St John, now a civil servant, observed some of the precautions being taken. On 23 August 1939, 'Men were working on trenches at Ealing Common, Acton Green Common and Stamford Brook Common … It looked as if the previous trenches had been filled in and they were having to dig new ones.' On 19 June 1940 he noted that a works in Acton was being guarded by 'two civilians wearing armlets and steel helmets, and carrying rifles'. St John would be glad of the shelters at Acton Common, for on 14 September 1940 he sheltered in one. Acton Council had been busy organising civil defence precautions. In October 1939, 835 personnel were registered for service, mostly in the auxiliary fire service, as air-raid wardens or in light rescue parties. By July 1940 there were home shelters for 17,500 people and public shelters for a further 4,885. Many of these shelters were constructed by Wimpey's.

The Blitz took its toll on Acton between September and November 1940. It was especially heavy in late September. Bombing in early 1941

125 Bomb damage at Princes Garden, 1940.

was far less extensive, but there were a number of fatalities. In all, the bombing caused 90 deaths and 130 serious injuries and 274 people sustained lesser wounds. Most streets had some damage to their buildings. As was the case nationally, 1942-3 saw relatively little bombing although, on 19 May 1943, a bomb hit the junction between Park Road North and Park Road East and four people were killed.

A couple of local diarists commented on the extent of the bomb damage. Alexander Goodlett wrote on 14 October 1940, 'In the afternoon, I walked to Acton Vale … and I saw that last night's

raid had done immense damage around the Vale and Chiswick.' St John noted on 26 September, 'At East Acton a house just north of the station had had something through the roof.' Four days later he observed that Gunnersbury Lane was cordoned off due to an unexploded bomb there. In October, some shops on the Uxbridge Road in Acton had been damaged and 'one had its upper floor destroyed by a direct hit'.

Just as victory seemed to be in sight, there were the attacks by flying bombs, the V1s and V2s, in the summer of 1944. Fortunately Acton

126 Bomb damage alongside the railway, c.1940.
127 Bomb damage on Perryn Road, 1940.

was unaffected by the latter, but seven of the former caused damage to property. East Acton Baptist church was all but wrecked on 22 June, and 20 houses in Fletcher Road were destroyed on the following day. Factories in Park Royal were damaged on 20 July. One Actonian recalled spending nights in a shelter under the Pensions Office at Bromyard Avenue: 'We used to dread moonlit nights as we knew the enemy had a clear

128 Men examine an unexploded anti-aircraft shell on Southfield Road playing fields, c.1940s.

view of everything when air raids took place. We were unable to wear night clothes as space was too confined and we had to make do with sleeping in bunks in our everyday wear.' The headmaster of Priory Boys' School noted in June 1944, 'pilotless plane bombing caused attendance to drop this week to 52.7%'. In the following month attendance was never above seventy.

Many of the schools which had evacuated their children to the West Country in September had brought them back before the war's end. At Acton Central School, there were two occasions in 1943 on which the shelters had to be used. Gas masks were inspected in April of that year. In the following year, two teachers suffered: Miss Chapman's

house was bombed and Mr Love, the French master, was killed in a raid in September 1944.

In all, 163 Actonians died in the raids, 290 were seriously hurt and 546 escaped with light injuries only – a total of 999 casualties of varying degrees, perhaps about three per cent of the resident population allowing for men being with the Forces and children being evacuated. Of the bombs which have been recorded individually, there were 369 high explosive bombs, two unexploded mines, 21 oil bombs, seven V1s and thousands of incendiary bombs.

After the fall of France, Anthony Eden, War Minister, made an appeal for men to join the Local Defence Volunteers (soon renamed the Home Guard), in order to oppose parachutists and saboteurs. At least 300 Acton men besieged the police station to enrol. Many were ex-servicemen. They drilled with rifles in the summer months and by October were training with machine guns and mortars.

As in the previous war, there was a pressing need to encourage savings. In November 1939 Acton formed a Savings Committee. There were 176 affiliated groups in April 1940; 250 by the following month. In the first three months, £145,507 worth of defence bonds, post office deposits and saving certificates had been bought. Schools and factories took part in these savings schemes. Acton Central School made £428 in the 'Salute the Soldier Week' in March 1944, whilst Priory Boys' School managed £366.

The London-wide War Weapons Week was 17-24 May 1941. The aim in Acton was to raise £320,000 worth of savings bonds in order to purchase a destroyer – to be named HMS *Acorn* after 'oak-town'. The week was designed to 'bring gaiety to Acton – gaiety and grim purpose'. There was a major parade of local uniformed

129 *Group on the steps of John Perryn School, c.1940s.*

organisations, complete with bands, a number of different sports events, variety performances and dances. It turned out to be a great success and a total of £552,274, or £10 per head of population, was raised. This was enough to buy a large destroyer, not the smaller one as first envisaged, and the residue went towards paying for the manufacture of a Spitfire.

Salvage was important, too. From June 1940 the Council's Salvage Sub-Committee began its drive to collect scrap metal. They decided not to take lamp posts unless the need was dire. In June 1940, 104 tons of scrap was collected and sold for £370. Apart from metal, paper, glass and bones were collected. In August of the following year it

was noted that enthusiasm for scrap collecting was on the wane. Fresh efforts, and a profile-raising parade of 500 people and three marching bands, enabled the council to meet its target of 100 tons of paper and also to collect treble the amount of iron.

Rationing was introduced almost at the outset of war, and the council operated a municipal piggery, the pigs being fed from scraps that Actonians deposited in special bins about the borough. The 'Dig for Victory' plea did not fall on deaf ears. The number of allotments in the borough rose from 150 in 1939 to 1,039 by 1941. Of these, 726 had been allocated by the council on playing fields, such as Acton Park, Acton Green, Southfield Road

Playing Field and land west of the old County School. Other land was lent by the Goldsmiths' Company.

St Mary's played a part in the conflict, as did the other churches. On 23 March 1940 there was the National Day of Prayer, at which the local Home Guard marched past the mayor and his colleagues. The mayor's chaplain told his congregation that the war and its aims were just. The Parish Hall and old Working Men's Club were taken over for civil defence use, but were damaged both by their new occupants and by enemy action. It was a sad time for St Mary's, as its congregation halved and it was unable to make any repairs owing to lack of funds.

Acton's many industries played an important part in the war effort. A 1961 borough guide boasted, 'In the Second World War, Acton's contribution was considerable'. Acton Bolt Ltd manufactured millions of bolts used in aircraft, which gave planes an extra safety factor. Wellington bombers flew home with much of their covering fabric shot away, but the essential structure held together by the bolts which allowed the planes to land safely. Wilkinson Sword Company made a special sword, 'the Sword of Stalingrad', which was presented at the Teheran Conference in 1943 to Josef Stalin, the Soviet leader, as a tribute to the defenders of Stalingrad. The mothballed aerodrome works were requisitioned at the height of the Battle of Britain in September 1940 by the Ministry of Aircraft Production and taken over by the De Havilland Aircraft Company. Here, fuselages for military aircraft and wings for the De Havilland Mosquito aeroplane were made. On completion these parts were sent elsewhere, largely to the De Havilland factory at Leavesden, for assembly. Aircraft parts were manufactured by Napier, too, mainly for the Typhoon and Tempest aircraft; mostly Sabre engines. Another local industry which switched to war work was CAV.

It was not all hard work and sacrifice during wartime, of course. The football team prospered after it was re-established in the 1940-1 season. Messrs Hollocks and Bond re-formed the club, running five teams, including one for schoolboys. The team gained admittance to the Middlesex Senior League in 1942 and used Roote's ground in East Acton Lane. Home games were played at Brentford's ground. In 1943 the club won the league and almost won the Middlesex Senior Cup, but lost 2-3 to Finchley. And, of course, there were the cinemas. Mr Goodlett noted going regularly in late 1939 to the Globe, but in the following year his fire-watching duties in London interrupted that routine.

There was a false dawn in the Savoy Cinema at East Acton on 2 May 1945 when an announcement declared, 'The Germans have surrendered'. The organist played God save the King as the audience danced in the aisles. Alas, as the deputy manager had to explain, the on-screen message was incomplete and should also have read 'in Italy'. The real thing was not far off, in any case. Victory in Europe was celebrated on 8 May 1945 in Acton as elsewhere. Bonfires were lit and bells rung; houses were decorated and parties held in the streets and in homes; children were given a couple of days off school; on the following Sunday there was a packed thanksgiving service at St Mary's, attended by the mayor and other civic dignitaries. Just over three months later, with the surrender of Japan on 15 August, the day in Acton got off to a noisy start with sirens and hooters being sounded as soon as midnight struck.

IX

Acton in the Fifties and Sixties

After the war, the task of reconstruction began. War had not caused much industrial damage and Acton's factories remained. New ones located here and others expanded, but a few were to depart by the 1960s. The Labour Council's main project in this era was the rebuilding of South Acton, not primarily because of enemy action but on account of its poor housing. Yet the strong civic pride of earlier decades seemed less apparent, especially when the borough's future as an independent political entity came into question.

If Acton became a town of industry in the '20s and '30s, this was still the case after the Second World War. In 1957 nearly three times as many employees lived outside the borough as inside it, and the population increased by about 20,000 on each working day. In 1954, according to County Council statistics, Acton boasted 399 factories and the highest industrial rateable value in the county, £115,531.

The variety of products was astounding. In 1961 the town produced 'Electric-meters and

130 *New factories in South Acton, 1963.*

motor cars, swords and shaving brushes, gyro compasses and golf clubs, not to mention ice cream'. A comment in the local press ran, 'Acton is the biggest industrial centre south of Birmingham … It is a sleek, well groomed, efficient hub of modern industrial activity.'

New firms established themselves after 1945. One was More O'Ferrall Studios, started in 1952, which undertook the production of signs and outdoor advertising and other display work. It was estimated that they produced 25,000 square feet of artwork per week. Green (Polyfoil) Ltd, a producer of aluminium decorations and kitchen foil, moved from Brentford to Acton in 1946. Other firms expanded their premises or diversified in this period. Acton Bolt Ltd, for example,

manufactured large quantities of high tensile fasteners for the engineering industry. Heinz employed 2,000 staff in 1949 and about 3,500 in 1964. Walls' new plant, at Atlas Road, was opened by the Duke of Edinburgh in 1958.

The importance of industry in Acton was recognised and fostered in two other ways. Firstly, the public library became a recognised centre for books and pamphlets on industrial and technical matters, including works on nuclear research; during the Cold War the reference librarian had to monitor the use of such works by eastern Europeans! Secondly, the Brunel College of Technology was opened in 1957. It sought to develop higher technological education so that the country would be able to compete successfully in an aggressive

131 Women at work in Dubilier Condensor Co., Victoria Road, c.1955.

132 D bank capacitors, ready for shipment from Dubilier Condensor Co., to France, 1950.

Other firms followed at the end of the decade. Factory spaces became vacant as high rents discouraged new occupants. Acton was not as attractive to industry as it once was, partly owing to road congestion, and there was a movement to locate industry further from large cities. Yet local unemployment was low, only 270 being registered as such in 1963.

Laundries were in decline in these years, though Acton still claimed to be the centre of the laundry industry; there were only 50 left in 1953. Industrial and hotel trade was meant to provide a new demand for laundry services, but the industry was fighting a losing battle. The increasing use of domestic washing machines, dry cleaners and laundrettes all acted against it. The first laundrette appeared in Acton in 1950 and more

world. Local firms sent students to the College for sandwich courses in order to study for the Diploma in Technology.

Outside commentators were not particularly impressed by Acton's appearance. Michael Robbins referred in 1953 to 'its undistinguished streets' and noted that 'the industrial district of North Acton presents a horrid example of the twentieth century doing its worst'. Two years earlier, one Brett-James had written of Acton as possessing 'a maze of railway lines, a tangle of sidings, engine sheds with the huge concentration of industry of Park Royal'.

Some firms moved away from Acton in these years. Napier's left in 1962 after it became more expensive to operate in London and subsidies were made available from the government for firms which located in the north of England and other districts.

followed. Another blow to the industry was the slum clearance in South Acton in the 1960s, which spelt the end of the old home of the industry. According to Mr Rowland, writing towards the

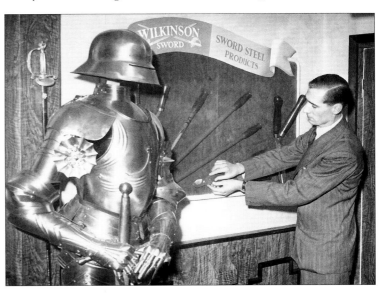

133 Wilkinson Sword factory, Southfields Road, 1950s.

134 Industrial Acton, with the CWS Jam factory in the centre, 1960s.

135 Derelict equipment in Crown Laundry.

end of the 20th century, with pardonable exaggeration, 'one would be less surprised to meet a mammoth or a dodo in South Acton than a laundry'. A century of Soapsud Island was virtually over.

One of the major concerns in Acton in this period was its status as a shopping centre. Apart from the High Street and Churchfield Road, trade was generally quiet, and in the High Street work was needed; in 1961 it was said to be too narrow and the shops unprepossessing. Many were derelict and shoppers went to Ealing or Uxbridge instead. In the 1960s a shopping precinct replaced the old buildings in the High Street, namely Suffolk and Lichfield House, as well as the abandoned adjacent cinema.

136 The Odeon Cinema and Acton High Street, 1950s.
137 Poore's shop on Acton High Street, 1950s.

Acton Council worked to provide replacement housing, some of which had been damaged or destroyed during the war. Between 1946 and 1965, 2,179 houses and flats were built, far more than the number built in 1918-39. In East Acton, the site of Manor Farm was used for flats around a garden in 1956. Developed by the Goldsmiths' Company, they were aimed at those on modest incomes. To the north of the Vale, six four-storey flats were built in the late 1940s, with delays due to bad weather and labour problems. Yet it was in South Acton that municipal rebuilding

138 Oldfield Housing Estate, c.1952.

was to be concentrated. This was hardly surprising because many of the houses had been built in the 1860s and were now considered inadequate for the brave post-war world. They were described as a 'shanty town' in 1958. Many only had two rooms and there were stories of families being divided among a number of properties. Four years later a builder remarked, 'South Acton is a jungle. Many of the houses aren't fit to live in. The area below Bollo Bridge Road is worse than an East End slum before the war. Now, today, the conditions are the worst in London.' A year earlier, a family living in

139 Buildings are demolished as part of the council's redevelopment scheme at the end of Junction Road, 1950s.

Osborne Road had decided to emigrate to Australia after 13 years during which they claimed the council had been neglectful of South Acton housing.

There had been talk of major redevelopment of South Acton since 1945. Parts of Junction Road, Palmerston Road and Stanley Road were acquired by compulsory purchase in 1951. The first block of flats to appear was on Vincent Road in 1954, a six-floor block of 34 flats. Houses on the western side of Hanbury Road were demolished in 1956 and replaced two years later by flats nine storeys high, costing £130,000 each. Flats, shops and garages on the east side soon followed. The older houses, between Bollo Lane, Avenue Road and Strafford Road, were demolished, with a few exceptions. In the 1960s two tower blocks of 22 storeys and three of 13 storeys were built. It was announced, perhaps optimistically, that 'An area which for so many years has been an eyesore will become one in which Acton can take some pride.'

140 Flats on Hardy Court, 1960s.
141 Redevelopment in South Acton, 1960s.

There seems no reason to mourn the passing of the small and overcrowded housing that once made up South Acton. Yet it is questionable whether the solution was much better. Materially it probably was, but as early as 1958 an Acton housewife declared, 'South Acton was a hell on Earth', as the flats were soon surrounded by rubbish and filth. By the 1970s there was discussion as to whether the tower blocks were a breeding ground for crime. The irony was that by the end of the century surviving terraced houses fetched high prices and some of the flats were being demolished.

Population declined after the war. From an estimated 67,621 in 1949, it fell to 64,800 eleven years later. To an extent this fall can be explained by people moving to the new towns (such as Bletchley and Hemel Hempstead, both of which attracted Acton residents) which were being built in the 1950s in the south of England. Yet Acton was still relatively overcrowded. In 1931, there had been an average of 30.2 people per acre; in 1951 this was 29.1 and in 1961, 28.3. This was still high by the standards of other boroughs in the county: of the 26, only four had a higher density in 1951,

142 *Flats in South Acton, 1960s.*

143 Trolley bus on Uxbridge Road, c.1960.

and only three by 1961. Furthermore, the number of households enjoying what were deemed basic amenities was relatively low by the standards of most other county boroughs. In 1951 only 43 per cent of Acton households had all five basic facilities (piped water, WC, fixed bath, kitchen sink and cooking stove), compared with a county average of 62 per cent. Only four other boroughs had lower totals. In 1961 the situation was better in absolute terms, but still relatively similar, 51.6 per cent having the basics when the county average was 73.1 per cent.

The exodus to new towns was partly offset by the influx of immigrants from overseas. In 1965 Acton's MP, Bernard Floud, remarked, 'There are large numbers of English and Irish and former Polish citizens, and there are now substantial numbers of coloured immigrants from the Common-

wealth.' Perhaps the most important group, as far as Acton was concerned, were the Poles. In 1961 there were 1,313 in Acton, the largest single immigrant group. Many Poles had fought with the British in the war and, unable to return home, decided to live in parts of west London, such as Hammersmith and Acton. Throughout the 1950s there were many notices in the local press by Poles wishing to become naturalised British citizens. In 1951 immigrants from the Commonwealth and the colonies numbered 570 and 158 respectively. By 1961 there were 820 Asians (including 549 Indians) and 356 Jamaicans, some of whom were expatriates. One result of their arrival was the emergence of a rather more exotic cuisine in Acton than had hitherto been known. The Koon Ying, a Chinese restaurant, was opened in Churchfield Road in 1961, swiftly followed by the Alighar Indian restaurant and the Cashbah Café, serving food suitable for Muslims, in 1963.

Reactions to the new arrivals varied. The education authorities instituted three English classes for the children of immigrants. A Conservative, Councillor Wicks, blamed them for housing problems and the growth of prostitution, but was told that it was his own party's Rent Act and unscrupulous landlords who were to blame. The Labour Party was generally more favourable, arguing that the newcomers were an asset to the economy. James Sparks said they should be welcomed. Local Liberals, although not motivated by prejudice, feared that unemployment and overcrowding would result if immigration were unchecked, and favoured restrictions.

Fears were probably fuelled by the attack, in 1960, on local dancer Carol Dourof by a coloured man, though this may have been an isolated incident. Others thought immigrants were being favoured regarding the allocation of housing, and that there should be a halt to immigration. On the other hand, the International Friendship League tried to encourage local people to welcome newcomers. The film *Samphire*, which was made in 1958 and explored contemporary attitudes to race relations, was partly shot in Acton.

Fear of racial violence followed the disturbances in nearby Notting Hill in 1958, yet the concerns seem to have been largely overstated. Some of the violence in this period was caused by 'teddy boys', who were often indiscriminate in their attacks. In 1960, a number of them, armed with makeshift weapons, beat up two coloured men on Acton Green, but this seems to have been the only reported incident of its kind. In 1954, a white railway worker had been attacked by them in Old Oak Lane. On the whole, reported racial violence was minimal, but clearly the issue of immigration was important.

Politically speaking, the constituency followed national trends. The socialist candidate, James Sparks, was elected in 1945 during Labour's great landslide victory and remained in post until 1959. When Harold Macmillan's Conservative party won a landslide victory, Mr Holland, a Conservative, was returned. At the 1964 election, Mr Floud of the Labour Party replaced him. The Liberals contested Acton for the first time in 1964, though without success, and a number of Communist candidates stood at council elections in this period, too, though none of them was ever elected. Acton Council was always solidly Labour in these years, with a very small Conservative opposition.

The period was perhaps the best of times for bus users. There were 16 routes through Acton in 1960 (an increase of five during the decade). They went westwards to Ealing, Hanwell, Southall, Hayes and Uxbridge. Northwards, one could travel to Harlesden, Hampstead Heath and South Harrow. To the east, destinations included Hammersmith, Shepherd's Bush, Oxford Circus, London Bridge and Liverpool Street. Finally, to the south one could visit Chiswick, Kew, East Dulwich and Wandsworth by bus. There was also the 'Green Line' coach service, running buses further afield to places such as Amersham, High Wycombe and Chesham. Trolley buses still operated until 1962 but were clearly in decline throughout the 1950s: in 1949 there had been five routes; by 1960 only two remained.

Another change in Acton's transport network affected the railways in 1947. Following the postwar phase of reorganisation, the Park Royal, North Acton and Old Oak halts on the Great Western line disappeared. However, the Central Underground Line branched north-west from East Acton towards Ruislip in the same year. The branch of the District line to South Acton from Acton Town was closed in 1959. Steam trains gave way to diesel trains in 1965.

There were proposals in 1963 that Acton Central station and South Acton station be made casualties of the Beeching Report, which

144 A bus travels past Goldsmiths' Arms, *East Acton, 1950s.*

145 Acton Central station was threatened with the 'Beeching Axe', 1963.

earmarked little used railway stations for closure, because the line from Richmond to Broad Street was under threat. Such moves would have increased journey times for commuters, and made them more expensive, too. Although the meeting to discuss action only attracted 45 people, there were letters of protest and a petition of 800 signatures. By 1965 the campaign was a success and the stations were saved.

Less easy to measure was the number of cars travelling in or through the borough, especially after the ending of petrol rationing in 1950, although local ownership undoubtedly rose. The numbers of road accidents could be calculated, however, and these seemed to be on the rise in the 1950s. In 1952 four died and 204 were injured; in the first nine months of 1953 this had risen to five deaths and 286 hurt. In 1956 there were 507 road injuries in Acton, and 516 in the following year (of

which nine were fatal). Road safety films were shown around the borough, but some felt both these and the road signs were ineffective.

With the advent of the Korean War in 1950, concerns over civil defence were back on the agenda. A local branch was formed in the same year and, by 1951, 132 people had enrolled. They used the old Fire Station on the High Street as their control centre. Although some (including communists and the local branch of the CND) criticised the organisation for being pointless in the face of a possible nuclear attack, it demonstrated its worth during the aftermath of the airliner crash on Southall in 1958.

Acton's football team, Acton Town, had mixed fortunes after 1945. They ceased using Brentford's ground when war ended and temporarily closed for several months, and in so doing lost players to professional clubs. However, in 1946, Messrs

146 Civil Defence workers practise at Wall's factory, 1950s.

Newson, Ellis and Bond negotiated with the Liverpool Victoria Assurance Company for use of their ground, and the club was able to enter the London League. Financial problems and the loss of more players to professional clubs helped ensure that Acton Town did badly in the 1947-8 league tables. In 1949 their position improved. New blood was brought onto the committee and the team finished the season near the top of the table.

With the increasing ownership of television sets, the great days of cinema were over. This was reflected in Acton by the closure of the Gaumont (as the Globe had been renamed in 1949) in 1959 and the closure of the Savoy three years later. Only three cinemas remained. A report in the local press in 1963 declared, 'as far as people and social life are concerned, Acton is dead, dismal and disinterested [*sic*]'. There might be 42 pubs, but there were only two cinemas and no dance halls. Perhaps this was because of the pull of the brighter lights of London, so easily reached by most of those who lived within its orbit.

Educationally there were changes, too. In 1954 Dr Smart, Director of Education, was asked to prepare a report on changes to secondary schooling in the borough, which was followed by a political clash. Conservatives feared (rightly) an end to the selective grammar schools; their Labour opponents, such as James Sparks MP, favoured such a move on the rather pious grounds that comprehensive education would raise all schools to the standards of the grammar schools. Acton County School, once the town's select establishment, became a mixed sex school in the 1950s and comprehensive in the following decade. On a happier note the Elms, Acton's only remaining 18th-century building, was taken over for educational uses in 1954 and considerably added to, and it became

Twyford High School three years later. It replaced the Central School, which closed in 1957. Bromyard Avenue Secondary Modern School opened in 1955. The Barbara Speake School for Performing Arts was established in 1946.

The provision of higher education was

147 Barbara Speake Stage School, class of 1964.

increased. In 1949 there were 410 full-time and 1,368 part-time students at the Technical College, mostly non-resident in the borough. Sandwich courses began in 1955, when there were about 350 teachers, mostly part-time, and almost 5,000 students, again mostly part-time. New buildings in Woodlands were used from 1956 (the County School having vacated the premises just before the war), and this was the origin of the Brunel College, later University of Technology. Many of the staff transferred to the new college, which taught engineering, chemistry, physics, electronics and mathematics.

Acton became associated with a number of celebrities from the world of show-business in the 1950s and 1960s. Sid James, a South African, lived in 35 Gunnersbury Avenue in the 1950s, before moving to Iver in Buckinghamshire in 1961. He was a well-known face in British TV dramas and films, and is best remembered for his roles in the low-budget, low-brow 'Carry On' comedies of the

148 *Brunel College, c.1960.*

149 *Multiculturalism at Rothschilds School, late 1960s.*

1960s. Of more international renown was the
Scottish actor, Sean Connery, who bought a large
house near Acton Park for £9,000 in 1962. At this
time he was becoming a major film star, mostly
because of his portrayal of James Bond. Connery
left Acton in 1967. Bill Owen, born in Acton in
1914, was a rising star in British TV from the 1950s.
His best-known role was as 'Compo' in 'Last of
the Summer Wine'. He occasionally returned to
his home town.

Acton was also the 'breeding ground' of a
number of young men who were to make their
names in popular music. Terry Nelhams, better
known as Adam Faith, was brought up in a council
flat in Acton Vale in the 1940s. In 1959 he shot to
stardom as a solo singer with the song 'What do
you want?' and became a teenage idol overnight.
He had begun his working life in a metal factory
in Acton. Then there were the youths who made
up The Detours, later The Who. Peter Townsend
and Roger Daltrey met at Acton Grammar School
in the late 1950s and formed a skiffle band. They
were later joined by John Entwhistle and Doug
Samdom, and the group then possessed two
guitarists, a drummer and a singer. In 1963 the
secretary of their fan club remarked, 'They have a
good sense of humour … and they can play very
good harmonies'.

Acton's days as a borough were numbered.
Talk of reform in London's local government was
abroad in the 1950s, and the trend was for a smaller
number of larger boroughs. Acton's population
was relatively small compared to its larger neighbours, Ealing, Hammersmith and Willesden. The
report of the Royal Commission in 1960
recommended that Acton, Chiswick and Brentford
should form a single unit for local government
purposes, a new borough of about 121,000 people.
The new borough would have increased powers,
that at present were in the remit of the Middlesex
County Council, and there were tensions between

150 Adam Faith, Acton's superstar of the 1960s.

the County Council and the borough councils.
Schools, traffic and finance would be dealt with
more at the level of the new boroughs.

Reactions of local people, where known, were
largely apathetic. According to the local press, such
proposals were 'greeted by a wave of indifference
from local people'. Most thought there would be
little or no change in their everyday lives. There
was very little enthusiasm except for those directly
involved in local government. The resigned nature
of many was summed up by Charles Hocking,
former borough librarian, who remarked, 'Acton,
in common with other places, must necessarily lose
some of its identity, but it is in the nature of things.
As far as local patriotism is concerned, it will be
rather sad, but there it is.'

However, by 1961 the idea had been dropped.
The Minister for Local Government announced
that the new boroughs would have to have popula-
tions of at least 200,000. The new possibilities
included Acton merging with Brentford, Chiswick
and Hammersmith, or with one of the larger
neighbours, Willesden or Ealing. Gerry Reynolds,
Acton's mayor, whilst recognising that 'There is

bound to be sadness that the borough of Acton will disappear', thought it would be beneficial because it would mean the larger boroughs had more power devolved to them. He believed Acton would probably merge with Hammersmith and Chiswick. *The Acton Gazette* thought this was likely too, because of the existing links with Bedford Park and Shepherd's Bush, in which case it was thought Hammersmith would be the name of the new borough owing to its size and because it was the first to be incorporated (in 1900).

By 1963 such speculation was over. Acton would be joined to Ealing and Southall in two years' time. The question remained what the new borough was to be called. There was reference to its new name being an amalgamation of the three existing names, one bizarre possibility being Elactall. This was denied by Alderman Turner, Ealing's mayor. Members of the joint committee of councillors from the three boroughs came to a decision. It was to be Ealing, and, oddly enough, it was the Acton councillors on that committee who made the suggestion. There was no opposition from the Southallians and, naturally, the Ealing councillors were delighted. The final meeting of Acton Council took place on 23 March 1965 and on 1 April 1965 it became part of the new London Borough of Ealing. Councillor Bill Hill recalled that the council's last meeting was not closed, but merely adjourned until further notice, though there seems no likelihood that Acton will ever regain its independence.

Since 1965, more of Acton's old heavy industries have moved elsewhere, and been replaced by the media and film trades. A supermarket has appeared to the west of St Mary's church and a small shopping centre, The Oaks, has opened in the High Street. Overall, though, the range of goods available in Acton is, generally speaking, smaller than what it was in the earlier 20th century. The Cottage Hospital and the Isolation Hospital have also been lost.

Yet Acton remains a popular place to live because of its good transport links. Some larger houses and old industrial sites have been converted into flats or new housing. The ethnic mix has broadened, and recently Acton has also become a favoured stopping point for young travellers from Australasia and South Africa. It is now more of a dormitory suburb than the town it once was. Attempts at urban regeneration are ongoing, notably by 'Action Acton'.

Acton, after 1965, was no longer its own master, although many matters were unaffected by this. This is not to say, however, that Acton remained the same. Many trends, already evident before 1965, continued in subsequent decades, not always for the best. The building of flats in South Acton continued, immigration continued (stimulating the National Front to field a candidate – who lost – in the 1968 by-election) and there was further relative decline in Acton as a shopping centre; local industries had varying fortunes and population fell. Yet, from the retrospect of the early 2000s, Acton survived. There seems no danger that it will disappear as a named entity with a meaning for both locals and visitors. Its neighbour, Shepherd's Bush, for instance, has never been a political unit, but most people know where and what it is. Acton has its own MP, though the constituency includes parts of Ealing and Shepherd's Bush. The many railway stations bearing the name Acton serve also to remind residents and travellers of Acton. Perhaps the motto of the former borough (doubtless taken from Eton's) should be the last word on the subject:

'Floreat Actona'

Sources

All are located at Ealing Central Library unless otherwise noted.

Primary
Acton Roll of Honour for the First World War
Acton Borough Guides (1908-61)
The Acton Gazette (1871-1965)
Acton Council Minutes, 1914-19, 1926.
The Acton Express, 1903
Acton Central School Log Book, 1905-57
Additional Manuscripts 61619 (British Library)
St Mary's Acton Girls' School, Log Book, 1910-19
Priory Boys' School log books, 1895-1950
Calendars of State Papers Domestic (16th and 17th centuries) [Public Record Office]
Calendars of Middlesex Quarter Sessions Records (16th and 17th centuries) [London Metropolitan Archives]
Middlesex Poll Book, 1802 [Public Record Office]
St Mary's Parish Magazines (1903)
Acton Vestry Minutes, 1775-1850
Mercurius Rusticus (1647)
Mercurius Politicus (1651) [British Library]
Anon, 'A Exact and True RELATION of the BATTELL Fought on Saturday last at ACTON' (1642)
Anon, 'The Valiant Resolution of the Seamen …' (1642) [British Library]
H. St John's diaries (1926, 1939-41)
A.K. Goodlett diary, XII (1940)
Dunckley, R., *South Acton, 1929-1939: A Personal View* (2003)
N. Keeble (ed.), *Autobiography of Richard Baxter* (1974)
Acton Churchwardens' Accounts, 1674-1817 [London Metropolitan Archives]
Acton Burial Registers, 1642-1721
Ordnance Survey maps, 1865-1970
Middlesex and Acton Directories, 1826-1955
Middlesex Census abstracts, 1921, 1931, 1951, 1961

Lord Clarendon, *History of the Rebellion* II (1849)

Brewer, J., *Beauties of Middlesex* V (1816)

Matthew, W., and Latham, R. (eds.), *The Diary of Samuel Pepys*, 1666, Vol. 7 (1972)

Secondary

Acton Historian (1990s)

Briggs, M., *Middlesex* (1934)

Chippendale, N., *The Battle of Brentford* (1991)

Goodlet, A.H., *The Story of Acton Aerodrome* (1978)

Gouge, I., *Acton: A Brief Outline of its Growth and Development* (1978)

Gouge, K., *A Study of Acton* (*c.*1970)

Harper Smith, T. and A., *Commonwealth Surveys of Acton* (nd)

    Acton Hearth Tax Assessments, 1664-1674 (1988)

    Soapsud Island (1988)

    Acton People, 1200-1700 (1989)

    Acton People, 1700-1900 (1990)

    The Uxbridge Road (1992)

    A Brief History of Acton (1993)

    East Acton Village (1993)

    Acton People, 3 (1992)

    Acton People, 4 (1995)

    Acton People, 5 (1996)

    The Rectors of Acton (1996)

Joliffe, P., *Acton and its History* (1910)

King Baker, W., *Acton, Middlesex* (1912)

Knights, D.C., *A Brief History of Electricity in Acton* (1987)

Knights, D.C., *Gas in Acton* (1989)

Lysons, D., *Environs of London* III (1795)

Mitchell, H., *Records and Recollections of Acton* (1913)

Oates, J.D., *Acton* (2002)

Robbins, M., *Middlesex* (1953, 2003)

Thomson, H., *Highways and Byways of Middlesex* (1909)

Thorne, J., *Handbook to the Environs of London, I* (1876)

Upton, D., *The Dangerous Years* (1993)

Vessey, A., *Napier Powered* (1997)

Victoria County History: Middlesex, Vol. VII (1987)

Walford, E., *Greater London, I* (1882)

Index

Page numbers in **bold** refer to illustrations.